P9-CEZ-718

D0015021

COOKING WITH
Bon Appétit

COOKING WITH
Bon Appétit

Italian Favorites

THE KNAPP PRESS
Publishers
Los Angeles

Bon Appétit® is a registered trademark of Bon Appétit Publishing Corp. Used with permission.

Copyright © 1987 by Knapp Communications Corporation

Published by The Knapp Press
5900 Wilshire Boulevard, Los Angeles, California 90036

All rights reserved. No part of this book may be reproduced, stored in a retrieval system or transmitted, in any form or by any means, electronic, mechanical, photocopying, recording or otherwise, without permission in writing from the publisher.

Library of Congress Cataloging-in-Publication Data

Italian favorites.

    (Cooking with Bon Appétit)
    Includes index.
    Contents: Antipasti—Soups—Pasta, grains, and breads—[etc.]
    1. Cookery, Italian.   I. Bon appétit.   II. Series.
TX723.I835   1987   641.5945   87-2599
ISBN 0-89535-184-6

On the cover (clockwise from lower left): *Calabrian Eggplant Salad; Celery Soup with Egg, Sausage and Cheese; Crisp-fried Salt Cod; Fried Pastry "Collars"; Linguine with Paprika Sauce.*

Printed and bound in the United States of America

10   9   8   7   6   5   4

❧ Contents

❧ Foreword

Dishes inspired by the cooking of Italy are more popular than ever. And why not? Italian food is very much like the Italians themselves: direct, charming and fun. This wide-ranging and spirited collection of recipes from *Bon Appétit* represents the best that country has to offer.

What you will discover in these easy-to-prepare recipes is that the essence of this cuisine is a loyalty to ingredients. Each cooking technique preserves the integrity of flavors—no disguises here. What you use should be of superior quality, with produce, meat, fish—everything—at their freshest. The saying, "Good cooking begins in the market," is certainly applicable to this collection of terrific dishes.

The food of Italy, with origins that are Greek, Roman, Byzantine and Oriental, is really the food of its region—from north to south, Piedmont, Lombardy, Veneto, Liguria, Emilia-Romagna, Tuscany, Umbria-The Marches, Rome-Lazio, Abruzzi-Molise, Naples, The Campania, Calabria-Lucania, Apulia, Sicily and Sardinia. Until 1861, they were independent and oftentimes at war with each other. Food is just as much a part of a culture as anything else, so it is interesting to see some of the most pronounced differences between regions extend to the cooking.

What these regions do have in common, though, is that the best food is made by home cooks. Eating is essentially a family affair, focusing on the midday meal. The structure is quite different from a typical American one. There are usually at least two principal courses, which are never brought to the table at the same time. Generally the dishes are presented in the order of antipasti; pasta, risotto or soup; fish, meat or poultry accompanied by at least one or two vegetable side dishes (which may develop into a separate course) and/or a salad; fruit and cheese or dessert and coffee.

Flexibility is the key here: Use this book to create your own traditional Italian meal or simply mix and match the recipes into your daily menus. Either way, you will enjoy exploring the diversity of this exciting cuisine.

1 ❦ *Antipasti*

In all of European gastronomy, there is nothing quite as seductive as Italian antipasti (hors d'oeuvres). An array of colors captivates the eye, and an explosion of tastes tantalizes the palate. Antipasti make a statement in and of themselves, as well as intimating what is to follow.

Italian antipasti, both hot and cold, are dominated by vegetables, cured meats, shellfish and cheese, all accented, of course, by oil, vinegar, aromatics, herbs and spices. Our collection of recipes encompasses a wide range of classic dishes, such as Roasted Peppers with Four Cheeses (page 9), Prosciutto and Melon with Cracked Coriander Seeds (page 2), Zucchini and Calamari Salad (page 7), Potato Caponata (page 2) (southern Italian mixed cooked vegetables) and Crostini Florentine Style (page 13) (chicken liver canapé). Our traditional regional antipasti include Mozzarella in Carrozza (page 11), deep-fried cheese sandwiches from Naples and Fried Pastry "Collars" (page 12) from Calabria.

Whether you decide to start your meal with something as simple as Anchovies with Parsley Sauce (page 2) or as lavish as Piedmontese Spinach and Cheese Sausages (page 10), you will be enchanted with these flavorful starters.

 Cold Antipasti

Prosciutto and Melon with Cracked Coriander Seeds

Serve the wine marinade as a refreshing drink to accompany this interesting variation on a classic appetizer.

6 servings

1 4- to 5-pound crenshaw, honeydew or casaba melon, peeled and cut into 24 slices
1 750-ml bottle dry Gewürztraminer (preferably Italian)

1 teaspoon whole coriander seeds
¼ teaspoon whole black peppercorns

24 very thin prosciutto slices
1 lemon, halved
   Olive oil

Place melon in nonaluminum bowl. Pour wine over. Refrigerate 1½ hours.

Heat heavy small skillet over high heat. Add coriander seeds and toss until slightly darkened, about 1½ minutes. Coarsely grind seeds and peppercorns in spice grinder or mortar.

To serve, drain melon, reserving wine. Arrange 4 prosciutto slices on each plate. Top with 4 melon slices. Squeeze lemon over melon. Sprinkle with spice mixture. Drizzle with olive oil. Pour wine marinade into glasses.

Anchovies with Parsley Sauce

8 to 10 servings

18 canned Italian salted anchovies
¼ cup minced fresh parsley
1 garlic clove, minced

⅓ cup (about) olive oil
   Cherry tomatoes
   Italian parsley

Rinse anchovies under cold water; pat dry. Arrange on platter. Combine ¼ cup parsley and garlic in small bowl. Whisk in enough oil in slow stream just to coat mixture. Drizzle over anchovies. Garnish with tomatoes and parsley. (*Can be prepared 3 days ahead.*) Serve at room temperature.

Potato Caponata

8 to 10 servings

4 pounds boiling potatoes

  Olive oil
2 teaspoons salt
2 large onions, coarsely chopped
1 large celery heart, diced
1 cup red wine vinegar
1½ tablespoons sugar

1½ cups Quick Tomato Sauce*
½ cup green olives, pitted and coarsely chopped
½ cup capers, drained and rinsed

Peel and dice potatoes. Cover with cold water and soak 5 minutes. Drain, rinse and drain again.

Heat 1 inch olive oil in heavy large skillet over medium-low heat. Add potatoes in batches (do not crowd) and cook 5 minutes. Increase heat to high and fry until golden brown, turning occasionally, about 8 minutes. Remove using slotted spoon and drain on paper towels. Sprinkle with salt. Pour off all but 1 cup oil from skillet. Add onions and celery and cook over medium-low heat until softened, stirring occasionally, about 10 minutes. Add vinegar and sugar and stir 2 minutes. Stir in potatoes and remaining ingredients. Serve at room temperature. (*Can be prepared 3 days ahead. Cool completely, cover and refrigerate.*)

*Quick Tomato Sauce

Makes about 1¹/₂ cups

¹/₄ cup olive oil
¹/₂ small onion, minced
2 garlic cloves, unpeeled, lightly crushed
3 cups drained and canned tomatoes, seeded and chopped

2 tablespoons minced fresh parsley
2 tablespoons minced fresh basil
1 teaspoon salt
1 to 2 teaspoons honey

Heat oil in heavy medium skillet over medium-high heat. Add onion and garlic and stir until aromatic, about 3 minutes. Discard garlic. Stir in tomatoes, parsley, basil, salt and 1 teaspoon honey. Cover partially and boil until almost all liquid evaporates, about 15 minutes. Add remaining honey if desired. (*Can be prepared 3 days ahead. Cool completely, cover and refrigerate. Bring to room temperature before using.*)

Italian Cured Meats

Cured meats are an indispensable part of antipasti as well as a popular way of flavoring a variety of cooked dishes. Here's a sampler of some of the most popular and commonly used meats.

Bresaola—Spiced, salted and air-dried, this cured meat can be made from a number of different cuts of beef but is most often made from the filet or loin. Thinly sliced and served with a dressing of virgin olive oil, chopped parsley, lemon and pepper, it makes for a simple yet elegant first course.

Coppa—This delicately spiced and cured pork shoulder is the ham most frequently used in cooking in Italian households. It is a bit fattier but a good, less expensive, substitute for prosciutto.

Mortadella—Made from various cuts of pork, beef or veal, or a combination, finely ground with seasonings and dotted with cubes of fat, this is smooth in texture with a delicate flavor. Mortadella comes from the city of Bologna, where it is accented with wine and coriander.

Pancetta—Made from the same cut of pork as bacon, pancetta is cured with salt and spices instead of smoked. It is most commonly used for flavoring in cooking but it is also a perfect addition to an antipasto selection.

Prosciutto—This delicately fragrant, dry-cured ham reigns king among Italian cured meats. Its sweet flavor makes it a perfect complement to melon and figs—a classic among antipasti.

Salami—Italian salamis, usually made of a mixture of pork and beef or veal, are well seasoned and smoked. Seasonings differ from region to region, but the more common include black pepper, red pepper, white or red wine and garlic. Their flavor may vary from mild to spicy.

Peppers Preserved in Vinegar

Excellent as part of an anti-pasto. The peppers can be sprinkled with olive oil and minced garlic if desired.

Makes about 1³/₄ pounds

4 1-inch pickling onions*
1³/₄ pounds red or combination of red and yellow bell peppers (ribs discarded), cut lengthwise into 1-inch strips
1 teaspoon salt

2 cups plus 2 tablespoons white wine vinegar
³/₄ cup water
1 oregano sprig or 2 teaspoons dried, crumbled

Make 3 slashes ¹/₃ inch deep in both ends of pickling onions. Place in 1¹/₂-quart jar. Add peppers and sprinkle with salt. Pour vinegar and water into jar, adding more water if necessary to cover peppers. Add oregano. Cover and marinate at room temperature 3 weeks before serving. (*Can be stored at room temperature up to 3 months.*)

*If unavailable, quarter 1 small onion.

Calabrian Eggplant Salad

Serve with plenty of crusty bread.

6 to 8 servings

2 medium eggplants (about 2 pounds total), unpeeled, ends discarded, cut lengthwise into ¹/₂-inch-thick slices
1 medium onion, cut into ¹/₃-inch-thick rings

20 slices Peppers Preserved in Vinegar (see above), drained

¹/₂ cup loosely packed whole fresh mint leaves
2 to 3 large garlic cloves, minced
  Salt and freshly ground pepper
6 tablespoons olive oil
3 tablespoons red wine vinegar

Halve eggplant slices lengthwise. Cook in large pot of boiling salted water until just tender, about 5 minutes. Remove with slotted spoon. Rinse with cold water and drain. Squeeze gently to remove excess water and pat dry. Blanch onion rings in same water 2 minutes. Drain thoroughly.

Alternate eggplant and preserved peppers in single layer on large platter. Top with onion. Sprinkle with mint, garlic, salt and pepper. Pour oil over vegetables; drizzle with vinegar. Let stand at room temperature 1 to 6 hours. Toss salad and serve.

Herbed Stuffed Eggs

8 servings

1¹/₃ cups fresh breadcrumbs
3 tablespoons butter
¹/₄ cup minced fresh herbs (parsley with sage, rosemary or basil)
8 hard-cooked small or medium eggs, peeled, halved and separated
  Salt and freshly ground pepper

²/₃ cup grated Parmesan cheese
²/₃ cup all purpose flour
2 eggs, beaten to blend

  Vegetable oil (for deep frying)

Preheat oven to 300°F. Spread breadcrumbs on baking sheet. Bake crumbs for about 10 minutes to dry.

Melt butter in heavy small skillet over low heat. Add herbs and stir until wilted, about 1 minute. Cool slightly. Mash yolks in small bowl. Stir in herb mixture. Season with salt and generous amount of pepper. Spoon herbed yolk mixture into egg whites.

Combine breadcrumbs and Parmesan in shallow bowl. Dip stuffed eggs in flour, then beaten egg; roll in breadcrumbs, coating thoroughly. Refrigerate uncovered at least 20 minutes. (*Can be prepared 6 hours ahead.*)

Heat oil in deep fryer to 360°F. Fry eggs in batches (do not crowd) until golden brown, turning occasionally, 3 to 4 minutes. Drain on paper towels. Sprinkle with salt and serve.

Spinach and Raisin Pie

A superb appetizer or main course.

6 to 8 main-course servings

Spinach Filling
2½ **cups spinach, stemmed**

¼ **cup olive oil**
¼ **cup minced onion**
3 **garlic cloves, minced**
6 **ounces black olives (preferably Kalamata), pitted and cut into ⅓-inch pieces**
½ **cup raisins**
¼ **to ½ teaspoon dried red pepper flakes**
Freshly ground pepper

Yeast Crust
2 **packages dry yeast**
1½ **cups warm water (105°F to 115°F)**
4½ **cups unbleached all purpose flour**

3 **tablespoons olive oil**
1 **tablespoon salt**

¾ **pound mozzarella cheese (preferably fresh), shredded**
6 **tablespoons olive oil**

For filling: Rinse spinach; shake off excess water. Transfer to Dutch oven. Cover and cook over low heat, stirring frequently, until just wilted, about 3 minutes. Rinse with cold water and squeeze dry. Chop coarsely.

Heat oil in heavy large skillet over low heat. Add onion and garlic and cook until soft, about 10 minutes. Mix in olives and raisins and cook 2 minutes, stirring frequently. Add spinach, red pepper flakes and pepper. Stir 5 minutes. (*Can be prepared 1 day ahead. Cover and refrigerate. Bring to room temperature before continuing.*)

For crust: Sprinkle yeast over ½ cup warm water in small bowl; stir to dissolve. Arrange 1½ cups flour in mound on work surface and make well in center. Add yeast to well. Using fork, gradually draw flour from inner edge of well into center until all flour is incorporated. Knead sponge until smooth and elastic, 8 to 10 minutes. (*Can also be prepared in processor. Knead 1 minute.*) Lightly flour large bowl and add sponge. Cover with towel. Let sponge rise in draft-free area until doubled, about 2 hours.

Arrange remaining 3 cups flour in mound on work surface and make well in center. Add raised sponge to well and pull to form well in sponge. Add remaining 1 cup water, 3 tablespoons oil and salt to well in sponge. Knead mixtures together until smooth and elastic dough forms, 8 to 10 minutes. (*Can also be prepared in processor. Knead 1 minute.*) Return to floured bowl. Cover with towel. Let dough rise in draft-free area until doubled in volume, about 1½ hours.

Mix cheese with 1 tablespoon oil. Add salt and pepper to taste.

Preheat oven to 400°F. Spread 3 tablespoons oil in bottom of 9 × 13-inch metal baking pan. Punch dough down. Cut into 2 pieces, one 1½ times larger than the other. Roll large piece out on lightly floured surface into 11 × 15-inch rectangle. Fit dough into prepared pan, covering bottom and sides. Brush with remaining 2 tablespoons oil. Spread filling in pan and sprinkle with cheese. Roll remaining dough out on lightly floured surface into 9 × 13-inch rectangle. Brush edges with water and place atop filling. Pinch top and bottom crusts together. Brush top of pie with water. Cut three 3-inch slits in top. Bake until well browned, about 35 minutes. Cool slightly. Serve pie warm or at room temperature.

Cheese Torta with Winter Pesto and Sun-dried Tomatoes

20 servings

Pesto
- 4 ounces frozen chopped spinach, thawed, drained and squeezed dry
- ½ cup chopped fresh parsley
- ⅓ cup freshly grated Parmesan cheese
- ¼ cup pine nuts
- 2 garlic cloves
- 1½ teaspoons dried basil, crumbled
- ½ teaspoon fennel seed
- ½ teaspoon salt
- ¼ teaspoon freshly ground pepper

- 1 10½-ounce jar sun-dried tomatoes packed in olive oil, drained (⅓ cup oil reserved)
- 2 8-ounce packages cream cheese,* room temperature
- 2 cups (4 sticks) unsalted butter,* room temperature
- 1 fresh parsley sprig
  Crackers, breadsticks and thin baguette slices

For pesto: Combine spinach, chopped parsley, Parmesan, pine nuts, garlic, basil, fennel, salt and pepper in blender or processor. Mix until smooth, stopping once to scrape down sides. With machine running, add reserved oil from sun-dried tomatoes (reserve tomatoes) in slow stream and continue mixing until very smooth.

Cut two 20-inch squares of cheesecloth. Dip into water and then squeeze dry. Place one square on top of other, then transfer to 5- to 6-cup charlotte mold or loaf pan, lining mold and allowing cheesecloth to drape over sides. Using electric mixer, beat cream cheese and butter until well blended. Set cheese mixture aside.

Set aside 2 whole sun-dried tomatoes. Finely chop remaining tomatoes in blender or processor using on/off turns. Arrange 2 whole tomatoes and parsley sprig in bottom of prepared mold. Using rubber spatula, spread ⅔ cup cheese mixture over tomatoes, creating smooth layer. Top with layer of ⅓ cup pesto, then another layer of ⅔ cup cheese mixture. Spread with half of chopped sun-dried tomatoes. Repeat layering, ending with cheese mixture. Fold edges of cheesecloth over top of torta. Refrigerate until firm, about 1 hour. Unwrap top of torta. Invert onto platter. Remove cheesecloth. Serve at cool room temperature with crackers, breadsticks and baguette slices. (*Can be prepared one week ahead, covered with plastic wrap and refrigerated. Bring to cool room temperature before serving.*)

*Two pounds mascarpone cheese can be substituted for cream cheese and butter. Soften cheese by stirring with wooden spoon; do not beat with electric mixer.

Shrimp in Tomatoes and Herbs

12 servings

- 3 quarts water
- 2 tablespoons red wine vinegar
- 1 tablespoon salt
- 1 carrot, coarsely chopped
- 2 pounds unshelled medium-size fresh shrimp
- 2 tablespoons olive oil

- 2 tablespoons olive oil
- 1 tablespoon butter

- 1 small onion, chopped
- 1 garlic clove, minced
- 1 cup peeled, halved and juiced Italian plum tomatoes (6 ounces)
- 2 to 3 teaspoons fresh lemon juice
- 1 teaspoon dried thyme, crumbled
- ¼ teaspoon salt
- ⅛ teaspoon freshly ground pepper

Combine water, vinegar, salt and carrot in large saucepan and bring to boil over high heat. Reduce heat until liquid is just shaking. Add shrimp and poach until pink, about 2 minutes. Drain shrimp well; peel and devein. Transfer to large bowl. Add 2 tablespoons olive oil and toss gently to coat.

Heat 2 tablespoons olive oil with butter in medium saucepan over low heat. Add onion and garlic, cover and cook until onion is translucent, about 10 minutes. Blend in tomatoes, lemon juice and thyme. Increase heat to medium and simmer until reduced and thickened to saucelike consistency, about 10 minutes. Pass sauce through food mill or press through strainer. Season with salt and pepper. Add sauce to shrimp and toss gently. Marinate shrimp in refrigerator several hours or overnight. Bring to room temperature before serving.

Zucchini and Calamari Salad

2 servings

2 6-ounce zucchini, cut into
  ¼-inch-thick rounds
1 teaspoon salt

1 tablespoon balsamic vinegar
2 teaspoons white wine vinegar
¼ teaspoon sugar
¼ teaspoon dried oregano,
  crumbled
⅛ teaspoon dried red pepper flakes
1 small garlic clove, crushed

1 tablespoon olive oil
  Salt and freshly ground pepper

1 pound small squid (about 6),
  cleaned and separated into bodies
  and tentacles

1 cup peanut oil

3 small garlic cloves, minced

Toss zucchini with salt in colander. Top zucchini with weight and let stand 30 minutes to drain off water.

Meanwhile, blend next 6 ingredients in small bowl. Whisk in oil. Season with salt and pepper. Let dressing stand 30 minutes to blend flavors.

Cut half of squid bodies into ¼-inch rings. Split open remaining bodies. Score with diamond pattern on both sides. Cut into 1 × 2-inch pieces.

Rinse zucchini; dry well. Heat peanut oil in heavy 10-inch skillet over medium-high heat. Add ¼ of zucchini and fry until golden brown, about 30 seconds per side. Remove using slotted spoon and drain on paper towels. Repeat with remaining zucchini.

Pour off all but 1 tablespoon oil. Set skillet over high heat. Add squid rings, pieces and tentacles and stir 2 minutes. Add minced garlic and stir until squid is tender and lightly browned, about 4 minutes. Transfer squid to bowl. Add zucchini. Remove garlic from dressing. Toss salad with dressing and serve.

Piedmontese Veal Antipasto

The flavor of this dish is enhanced by the palest pink veal, olive oil and well-aged imported Parmesan cheese. Allow each guest to squeeze lemon over meat just before eating.

6 servings

½ pound firm white mushrooms, wiped with damp towel, minced
2⅔ pounds lean veal shoulder (trimmed of all fat and sinew), finely ground
½ cup olive oil
3 large garlic cloves, minced
4 to 5 tablespoons freshly grated Parmesan cheese

1 tablespoon salt
Freshly ground pepper
12 1-inch mushroom caps, thinly sliced
½ cup Parmesan cheese slivers (use vegetable peeler)
Cornichons, pickled pearl onions and capers (optional garnish)
3 lemons, quartered

Roll mushrooms in clean towel and squeeze gently to remove excess moisture. Combine mushrooms and veal in large bowl and mix well. Blend in oil, garlic, Parmesan, salt and pepper. Mound mixture attractively in center of large serving platter. Sprinkle sliced mushroom caps and Parmesan slivers over top. Garnish with cornichons, pickled pearl onions and capers, if desired. Serve with lemon wedges.

Country Pork and Veal Pâté

For best flavor, prepare the bacon-wrapped pâté two days before serving.

8 to 10 servings

1 pound sliced bacon
¾ pound well-chilled boneless pork loin, cut into 1-inch pieces
½ pound well-chilled boneless veal, cut into 1-inch pieces
4 ounces well-chilled pork fat, cut into 1-inch pieces
2 tablespoons (¼ stick) butter
1 small onion, chopped
1 medium garlic clove, minced
½ pound chicken livers
¼ cup fresh breadcrumbs

¼ cup minced fresh parsley
2 eggs, beaten to blend
½ cup whipping cream
¼ cup brandy
1 teaspoon salt
1 teaspoon freshly ground pepper
½ teaspoon freshly grated nutmeg
¼ teaspoon ground allspice

3 ounces sliced ham, cut lengthwise into ½-inch-wide julienne
½ cup shelled pistachios

Blanch bacon in large pot of boiling water 3 minutes. Drain and pat dry. Line 8½ × 4½ × 2½-inch glass loaf pan with bacon, letting ends extend over sides of pan. Refrigerate pan.

Coarsely chop pork, veal and pork fat in batches in processor, using on/off turns. Transfer to large bowl. Melt butter in heavy large skillet over low heat. Add onion and garlic and cook until soft, stirring occasionally, about 8 minutes. Increase heat to medium and add livers. Cook until springy to touch, stirring frequently, about 4 minutes. Puree liver mixture in processor until smooth. Add to meats. Blend in breadcrumbs and parsley. Mix in all remaining ingredients except ham and shelled pistachio nuts.

Preheat oven to 350°F. Spread half of pâté in prepared loaf pan. Alternate ham and pistachios in lengthwise rows atop pâté. Add remaining pâté, smoothing top. Fold bacon ends in over pâté. Tap pan on counter to settle filling. Cover pan with double layer of foil. Tie string around edges to secure. Place loaf pan in baking pan. Pour enough boiling water into baking pan to come halfway up sides of loaf pan. Bake pâté until juices run yellow and thermometer inserted in center registers 160°F, about 2½ hours. Remove from water bath. Cool slightly. Place heavy object atop pâté. Refrigerate 2 days, removing weight after 4 hours. Let pâté stand at room temperature 30 minutes before serving.

🍎 *Hot Antipasti*

Pine Nut-stuffed Mushrooms

8 servings

2²/₃ cups fresh breadcrumbs

3 tablespoons butter
3 tablespoons minced shallot
16 medium mushrooms, stems
separated and finely chopped
Salt and freshly ground pepper
3 tablespoons plus 1¹/₂ teaspoons
chopped toasted pine nuts
Freshly grated nutmeg

¹/₃ cup minced fresh Italian parsley
²/₃ cup all purpose flour
2 eggs, beaten to blend

Vegetable oil (for deep frying)

Preheat oven to 300°F. Spread breadcrumbs on baking sheet. Bake crumbs for about 10 minutes to dry.

Melt butter in heavy small skillet over low heat. Add shallot and cook until soft, stirring occasionally, about 6 minutes. Add mushroom stems, salt and pepper. Increase heat to medium and cook until mushrooms are brown, stirring frequently, about 8 minutes. Add pine nuts and stir 1 minute. Add nutmeg. Cool slightly. Press filling into mushroom caps, leveling tops.

Combine breadcrumbs and parsley in shallow bowl. Dip each mushroom in flour, then egg; roll in breadcrumbs, coating thoroughly. Refrigerate uncovered at least 20 minutes. (*Can be prepared 6 hours ahead.*)

Heat oil in deep fryer to 360°F. Fry mushrooms in batches (do not crowd) until brown, turning occasionally, 3 to 4 minutes. Drain on paper towels. Sprinkle with salt and serve.

Roasted Peppers with Four Cheeses

8 servings

4 small red bell peppers, halved and
seeded, stems intact
4 small green bell peppers, halved
and seeded, stems intact

³/₄ pound ricotta cheese, drained
¹/₂ pound mozzarella cheese, grated
¹/₄ pound feta cheese, crumbled
5 tablespoons freshly grated
Parmesan cheese
¹/₄ cup minced fresh parsley

¹/₄ cup minced red onion
1 tablespoon minced drained capers
1¹/₂ teaspoons freshly ground pepper
1¹/₂ teaspoons dried basil, crumbled
1¹/₂ teaspoons dried oregano,
crumbled
10 anchovy fillets, drained

8 grape leaves or small
lettuce leaves

Char peppers over gas flame or in broiler until blackened but still firm. Cool peppers completely. Peel off skin.

Preheat oven to 400°F. Mix remaining ingredients except anchovies and grape leaves in large bowl. Mash 2 anchovies and add to cheese mixture. Mound in peppers. Arrange in baking dish. Bake until heated through and bubbly, about 20 minutes.

Line platter with grape leaves. Top with peppers. Halve remaining anchovy fillets. Set one atop each pepper and serve.

Melt-in-the-Mouth Eggs

6 servings

6 hard-cooked eggs
¹⁄₃ cup freshly grated Parmesan cheese
3 tablespoons Béchamel Sauce*
Freshly grated nutmeg
Salt and freshly ground pepper

All purpose flour
1 egg, beaten to blend
Seasoned breadcrumbs

Vegetable oil (for deep frying)

Halve eggs lengthwise and remove yolks. (Keep halves in matching pairs.) Mash yolks in medium bowl. Mix in Parmesan, Béchamel Sauce, nutmeg and salt and pepper. Divide mixture among halves, filling each to rim and smoothing evenly. Press halves together to re-form eggs. Roll each egg in flour, shaking off excess. Dip in beaten egg, then roll in breadcrumbs, covering completely. Arrange on baking sheet. Chill 30 minutes. (*Can be prepared 1 day ahead to this point. Bring to room temperature before continuing.*)

Heat oil in deep fryer to 375°F. Fry eggs in batches until golden brown, 8 to 10 minutes. Drain on paper towels. Serve eggs immediately.

*Béchamel Sauce

Makes about ¹⁄₂ cup

1¹⁄₂ teaspoons butter
2¹⁄₄ teaspoons all purpose flour

¹⁄₂ cup milk
Salt and freshly ground pepper

Melt butter in heavy medium saucepan over medium-low heat. Whisk in flour and cook 3 minutes. Remove from heat. Gradually whisk in milk until smooth. Return to medium heat and stir until sauce thickens and comes to boil, about 5 minutes. Boil 10 seconds. Season with salt and pepper.

Piedmontese Spinach and Cheese Sausages

12 servings

1 pound fresh spinach, stemmed
1¹⁄₃ cups dried breadcrumbs
1 cup plus 2 tablespoons ricotta cheese
¹⁄₂ cup freshly grated Parmesan cheese
4 eggs, beaten to blend
2 medium garlic cloves, finely minced
¹⁄₂ teaspoon salt

5 cups chicken stock
¹⁄₂ cup all purpose flour
¹⁄₂ cup (1 stick) butter, melted
2 teaspoons dried sage, crumbled
Freshly grated Parmesan cheese
Parsley sprigs (garnish)

Wash spinach thoroughly; shake to remove excess water. Transfer spinach to Dutch oven. Place over low heat, cover and cook until wilted, stirring frequently, about 5 minutes. Drain spinach well and squeeze dry. Chop spinach coarsely. Transfer to large bowl. Blend in crumbs, cheeses, eggs, garlic and salt; mixture should be very firm. Form mixture in ¹⁄₂ × 2-inch sausages. (*Sausages can be prepared 1 day ahead. Cover and refrigerate.*)

Preheat oven to 350°F. Generously butter large baking dish. Bring stock to rapid boil in large saucepan. Roll sausages in flour, shaking off excess. Carefully add sausages to stock in batches of 15 to 20 and cook until sausages float to top, about 2 minutes. Transfer to prepared dish using slotted spoon. (*Sausages can be prepared ahead to this point and set aside at room temperature.*) Pour melted butter over sausages. Sprinkle with sage. Bake until warmed through, about 10 minutes. Transfer to individual plates. Sprinkle with Parmesan cheese. Garnish with parsley and serve immediately.

Mozzarella in Carrozza

4 servings

Milk
8 ½-inch-thick slices Italian Country Bread (see page 45) or French bread, crusts trimmed if desired
4 slices mozzarella, Bel Paese or Fontina cheese, cut about same size as bread

All purpose flour
1 egg lightly beaten with pinch of salt
Olive oil

Pour milk into shallow bowl. Dip bread slices into milk just to dampen. Divide cheese among 4 slices of bread; top with remaining bread. Dust sandwiches with flour. Dip all sides into beaten egg. Pour olive oil into large skillet to depth of ¼ inch. Place over medium-high heat. When oil is hot, add sandwiches and fry until golden, turning once. Drain thoroughly on paper towels and serve immediately.

Polenta Appetizers

8 servings

4 cups water
1 tablespoon salt
1 cup polenta (Italian cornmeal)*

3 ounces very thin pancetta** slices, halved

3 ounces Emmenthal cheese, grated
3 ounces Italian Fontina cheese, grated
½ cup grated Parmesan cheese

Bring water to boil over medium heat. Add salt. Gradually stir in polenta and cook until mixture is thick and pulls away from bottom and sides of pan, stirring frequently, about 40 minutes. Cook 30 seconds without stirring. Pour onto buttered 12 × 16-inch baking sheet, spreading evenly. Smooth top with moistened spatula. Let polenta cool until firm.

Butter another baking sheet. Using 3-inch cutter or glass, cut out as many polenta rounds as possible. Invert rounds onto prepared sheet. (*Can be prepared 2 days ahead, covered and refrigerated.*) Top each round with piece of pancetta. Combine cheeses. Sprinkle generously over pancetta. (*Can be prepared 8 hours ahead and refrigerated.*)

Preheat oven to 400°F. Bake until cheese is melted and polenta is browned, about 8 minutes. Cool slightly before serving.

*Available at Italian markets. Regular yellow cornmeal can be substituted.
**Pancetta, unsmoked bacon cured in salt, is available at Italian markets.

Fried Pastry "Collars"

Choose your favorite fillings for these appetizers, using one or more in each.

Makes about 26

1 package dried yeast
1 cup (about) warm water
(105°F to 115°F)
3 cups unbleached all purpose flour

½ cup lard, room temperature
2 teaspoons salt

Fillings
  Anchovies, rinsed and patted dry

Thinly sliced prosciutto
Thinly sliced provolone cheese
Kalamata olives, pitted and
  coarsely chopped
Crisp-fried diced pork fat

Lard or vegetable oil
  (for deep frying)

Sprinkle yeast onto ½ cup warm water in small bowl; stir to dissolve. Arrange 1½ cups flour in mound on work surface and make well in center. Add yeast to well. Using fork, gradually draw flour from inner edge of well into center until all flour is incorporated. Knead sponge until smooth and elastic, 8 to 10 minutes. (*Can also be prepared in processor. Knead 1 minute.*) Lightly flour bowl and add sponge. Cover bowl with towel. Let sponge rise in warm draft-free area until doubled in volume, about 2 hours.

Arrange remaining 1½ cups flour on work surface and make well in center. Add raised sponge to well, then pull to form well in sponge. Add lard and salt to well in sponge. Work mixtures together, using hands, adding enough remaining water to make soft dough. Knead until smooth and elastic, 8 to 10 minutes. (*Can also be prepared in processor. Knead 1 minute.*) Return to floured bowl. Cover with towel. Let dough rise in draft-free area until doubled in volume, about 1½ hours.

Punch dough down. Pinch off 1½-inch balls of dough. Roll one piece into 3½ × 4½-inch rectangle. Arrange filling over dough. Starting at 1 long edge, roll up loosely jelly roll fashion. Form into ring by pinching ends together. Set on floured cloth. Shape and fill remaining dough. (*Can be prepared 3 hours ahead. Cover and refrigerate. Do not bring to room temperature.*)

Melt lard in deep skillet to depth of 2 inches and heat to 350°F. Add dough in batches (do not crowd) and cook until light brown, about 45 seconds on each side. Drain on paper towels. Serve pastries immediately.

For variation, roll unfilled dough into short cylinders. After deep-frying, arrange in single layer on baking sheet and drizzle with ¼ cup warmed honey. Sprinkle with ¼ cup diced candied fruit.

Fettunta with Swiss Chard

2 servings

2 tablespoons olive oil
1 garlic clove, minced
1 bunch Swiss chard (about
  ¾ pound),* rinsed, patted dry
  and coarsely chopped (discard
  any tough stalks)

Salt and freshly ground pepper
2 slices Grilled Garlic Bread (see
  page 48), each about 4½ × 8 inches

Heat olive oil in 10-inch skillet over medium-high heat. Add garlic and sauté 1 to 2 minutes (do not brown). Stir in chard. Reduce heat to medium, cover and cook until tender, about 3 minutes, stirring frequently. Season with salt and pepper. Spread mixture over Grilled Garlic Bread. Serve immediately.

*Spinach can be substituted but flavor will be milder. Leaves should be left whole. Drain well before spooning onto bread.

Eggplant Crepes Filled with Ricotta Cheese

6 to 8 servings

Eggplant
- ½ cup (or more) vegetable oil
- 1 medium unpeeled eggplant, cut lengthwise into ¼-inch-thick slices
- 1 cup all purpose flour seasoned with salt and pepper
- 3 eggs, beaten to blend

Tomato Sauce
- 3 tablespoons olive oil
- 1 small onion, minced
- 6 garlic cloves, coarsely chopped
- 2 12-ounce cans Italian plum tomatoes (undrained)
- 2 tablespoons chopped fresh basil
- 1 teaspoon sugar
- 1 large bay leaf

Pinch of dried oregano, crumbled
Salt and freshly ground pepper
- 1 cup thinly sliced mushrooms

Filling
- 1 pound whole milk ricotta cheese
- ½ cup freshly grated Romano cheese
- 2 eggs
- 3 tablespoons chopped Italian parsley
- 2 garlic cloves, minced
Salt and freshly ground pepper
- ½ pound mozzarella cheese
Freshly grated Romano cheese

For eggplant: Heat ½ cup oil in heavy large skillet over medium-high heat. Dredge eggplant in flour, shaking off excess. Dip in egg, allowing excess to drip back into bowl. Dredge in flour, shaking off excess. Add eggplant to skillet in batches and brown well on both sides, about 5 minutes per side, adding more oil if necessary. Remove using slotted spatula and drain on paper towels. Cool completely.

For sauce: Heat olive oil in another heavy large skillet over medium heat. Add onion and garlic and cook until onion is lightly browned, stirring occasionally, about 7 minutes. Add tomatoes with liquid, basil, sugar, bay leaf, oregano, salt and pepper and simmer until thickened to saucelike consistency, stirring frequently, 20 to 30 minutes. Add mushrooms and cook until just tender, about 5 minutes.

For filling: Mix 2 tablespoons tomato sauce and all filling ingredients in large bowl. Cover and chill until ready to use.

To assemble: Preheat oven to 375°F. Divide filling among eggplant slices, spreading evenly. Roll each up into cylinder. Arrange "crepes" seam side down in baking pan. Cut mozzarella cheese into same number of slices as crepes. Top each crepe with slice of cheese. Bake 10 minutes. Spoon sauce over. Sprinkle with grated Romano. Bake 5 minutes. Serve immediately.

Crostini Florentine Style

Makes about 1½ cups

- 3 cups chicken stock (not highly salted) or water
- 1 pound chicken livers
- 8 generous tablespoons capers, drained

- 12 anchovy fillets

Thin triangles of Italian Country Bread (see page 45) or French bread, plain or toasted

Bring stock or water to boil in 2-quart saucepan. Add chicken livers and poach over medium heat until barely pink inside, 3 to 5 minutes, removing livers with slotted spoon as they are done (*do not overcook*). Reserve liquid.

Chop capers and anchovies finely in processor or blender. With machine running, drop chicken livers through feed tube several at a time and puree until smooth, adding enough reserved poaching liquid to make thick, creamy spread. (*Can be prepared ahead to this point, covered and refrigerated.*)

Just before serving, transfer mixture to small saucepan. Place over low heat until just warmed through (not hot). Spoon into serving dish or crock. Accompany with bread or toast.

Squid-stuffed Squid

Intriguingly flavored phyllo pockets.

8 servings

8 large squid (about 1 pound total), cleaned
4 teaspoons olive oil
2 large garlic cloves, coarsely chopped
5 whole sun-dried tomatoes in oil, drained and quartered
1/8 teaspoon dried red pepper flakes
3 tablespoons dry white wine

4 teaspoons minced fresh cilantro
2 tablespoons plus 2 teaspoons dried breadcrumbs

4 phyllo pastry sheets
1/2 cup (1 stick) unslated butter, melted
Fresh cilantro sprigs

Cut fins off squid; set 4 largest bodies aside. Cut remaining squid bodies into 1/2-inch-thick rings. Halve all fins and tentacles. Heat oil in heavy medium skillet over low heat. Add garlic and stir 1 minute. Add squid rings, fins and tentacles. Increase heat to medium and stir until opaque, about 2 minutes. Add tomatoes and pepper flakes. Increase heat to medium-high and stir until any liquid evaporates. Add wine and stir until evaporated. Cool.

Chop squid mixture and minced cilantro in processor until texture of very coarse breadcrumbs, using on/off turns. Incorporate breadcrumbs using 2 on/off turns. Transfer to bowl. Cool to room temperature.

Fill reserved squid with breadcrumb mixture. Close each with toothpick. Bring water to boil in bottom of steamer. Arrange squid on steamer rack Cover and steam until squid turn opaque, about 3 minutes. Cool completely. (*Squid can be prepared 1 day ahead and refrigerated.*)

Preheat oven to 400°F. Brush 1 phyllo pastry sheet with melted butter (keep remainder covered with damp towel to prevent drying). Fold in half crosswise and brush with butter again. Place 1 squid at 1 short end, removing toothpick. Roll squid up in pastry, folding in ends. Place on baking sheet. Cut pastry crosswise in center almost all the way through. Brush pastry with butter. Repeat with remaining squid and pastry sheets. Bake until golden brown, about 10 minutes. Cut pastries in half. Transfer to platter. Garnish with cilantro sprigs and serve.

2 ❧ Soups

For most Americans, the ubiquitous minestrone is the first and last word in Italian soup. What a shame. But it's not without reason. The first course in an Italian meal is almost always pasta, risotto or soup and Italy's impressive soups are often unfairly overshadowed by the popularity and variety of pasta. (Don't forget, pasta lovers, in many cases you can eat your soup and have your pasta too—because the soups often contain pasta.) In this chapter you can discover—or rediscover—some of Italy's best-known and best-loved soups.

Italian soups fall, roughly speaking, into three categories, and in our assortment of recipes we offer representatives of each one. The first is a broth utilizing a meat, chicken or vegetable base, such as Chicken Broth with Italian Greens (page 16). The second is one thickened with fresh or dried vegetables or beans, rice or pasta, such as Chick-Pea, Tomato and Mint Soup (page 18), Tuscan Bean Soup (page 19) or Red Pepper Soup with Bruschetta (page 18). And the third is broth with pasta or rice floating in it, such as Tortellini in Broth (page 16). What transcends all three categories is the generous use of grated Parmesan or Romano cheese, stirred in for added thickness and flavor. Some of these soups make a delicate first course; some are robust enough to be a meal. All, without a doubt, are delicious.

Tortellini in Broth

If any filling remains, it can be used as a stuffing for omelets or peppers.

6 to 8 servings

2 cups all purpose flour
2 eggs

1 tablespoon butter
1 tablespoon vegetable oil
½ pound skinned boned chicken breast, patted dry and cubed
2 ounces mortadella
1 small egg
Pinch of freshly grated nutmeg

8 cups chicken stock (preferably homemade)
Freshly grated Parmesan cheese (optional)

Place flour on work surface and make well in center. Break eggs into well and blend with fork. Gradually draw small amount of flour from inner edge of well into eggs with fork, stirring constantly until eggs have absorbed as much flour as possible. (Eggs may not absorb all of flour.) Gather dough into ball. Scrape hard bits from work surface and discard. Lightly flour work surface and hands. Knead dough until smooth and elastic, adding as much of remaining flour as necessary to make dough that is firm but not hard, about 10 minutes. Wrap in plastic. Let stand at room temperature for 30 minutes. (*Can be prepared 1 day ahead and refrigerated.*)

Melt butter with oil in heavy small skillet over medium heat. Add chicken and sauté 1 minute. Transfer to processor. Add mortadella, egg and freshly grated nutmeg and chop finely using several on/off turns.

Cut dough in half. Rewrap half in plastic to prevent drying. Roll remainder out as thinly as possible on lightly floured surface. (*Dough can also be rolled out in hand-cranked pasta machine.*) Cut out 4-inch rounds using tortellini cutter or glass. Place scant ½ teaspoon filling in center of round. Moisten edge with water. Fold in half over filling, pressing edges to seal. Pinch 2 pointed edges together, forming little peaked cap. Repeat with remaining rounds. Arrange on kitchen towel-lined baking sheet, spacing so sides do not touch. Repeat with remaining dough and filling. (*Can be prepared 1 day ahead, covered with another towel and chilled, or dried at room temperature and frozen up to 3 months.*)

Bring stock to boil in large saucepan. Add tortellini and cook until just tender but firm to bite (al dente), about 3 minutes for fresh (depending on dryness), 10 to 12 minutes for frozen. Serve immediately. Pass grated Parmesan cheese if desired.

Chicken Broth with Italian Greens

Pass a pepper mill at the table to add the finishing touch to this starter.

8 servings

¼ cup corn oil
3 pounds chicken wings or backs

1¼ pounds onions, finely chopped
9 ounces carrots, finely chopped
1 bunch parsley, stems only
8 garlic cloves
1 tablespoon dried marjoram, crumbled
1 teaspoon dried thyme, crumbled
2 bay leaves

12 cups chicken stock (preferably homemade)
12 whole black peppercorns
Salt
4 cups finely shredded mixed Italian salad greens (such as escarole, arugula, romaine or spinach)

Heat oil in heavy large pot over medium-high heat. Pat chicken dry. Add to pot (in batches if necessary) and brown well on all sides, 20 minutes.

Add onions, carrots, parsley stems, garlic and herbs to pot. Reduce heat to medium-low, cover and cook until vegetables are lightly colored, stirring occasionally, about 25 minutes.

Add stock (and water if necessary to cover ingredients) and peppercorns to pot and bring to boil. Reduce heat, cover and simmer 2 hours, stirring occasionally and skimming surface. Cool chicken broth slightly.

Strain broth, pressing on solids to extract as much liquid as possible. Measure broth. If more than 2 quarts, boil until reduced to that amount. Cool broth completely. Chill overnight.

Degrease broth. Transfer to saucepan and bring to boil. Season with salt. Divide greens among bowls. Ladle broth over. Serve immediately.

Cabbage Soup with Fontina

4 to 6 servings

12 large savoy cabbage leaves

¼ pound pancetta, cut into ⅓-inch cubes

6 slices Italian bread, ½ inch thick
6 slices prosciutto, ¹/₁₆ inch thick
¼ pound Fontina cheese, thinly sliced

1 quart beef, veal or chicken stock (or combination), preferably homemade
Freshly grated nutmeg
Freshly ground pepper
6 tablespoons (¾ stick) butter

Blanch cabbage leaves in boiling salted water; drain. Cut away thick center core.

Preheat oven to 325°F. Sauté pancetta in deep 6-cup flameproof baking dish over medium heat until barely cooked. Remove from heat. Arrange layer of cabbage leaves over pancetta. Top with some of bread slices, prosciutto, cheese and enough stock to cover. Sprinkle with nutmeg and pepper. Repeat layering using remaining ingredients, ending with cheese. Dot with butter. Cover and bake 20 minutes. Remove cover and continue baking until brown and bubbly, 20 minutes. Let stand several minutes before serving.

For individual servings, sauté pancetta in heavy medium skillet over medium heat until barely cooked. Divide evenly among 6 ovenproof soup crocks or deep bowls. Layer and bake according to instructions above.

Celery Soup with Egg, Sausage and Cheese

This fresh-tasting soup has a trio of intriguing garnishes.

6 servings

¼ cup olive oil
4 cups ¼-inch-thick slices celery (about 1 pound)
2 tablespoons minced celery leaves
6 cups boiling beef broth (preferably homemade)
Freshly ground pepper

6 ½-inch-thick slices Italian bread, baked until light brown
Olive oil

3 hard-cooked eggs, chopped
3 ounces soppressata* or other dried sausage, cut into ⅛-inch cubes
3 ounces caciocavallo cheese or provola cheese,** cut into 2 × ⅛-inch julienne
Salt (optional)
Freshly grated Romano cheese
Fresh lovage or celery leaves

Heat oil in heavy large saucepan over medium-low heat. Add celery and 2 tablespoons celery leaves and cook until tender, stirring occasionally, about 15 minutes. Add boiling broth and pepper. Cover partially and simmer 20 minutes to blend flavors.

Brush bread with olive oil and place 1 slice in each bowl. Top each with egg, sausage and caciocavallo cheese. Taste soup and season with salt if desired. Ladle soup into bowls. Sprinkle generously with pecorino cheese and top with lovage. Serve immediately.

*Dried Italian sausage flavored with ginger. Available at Italian markets.
**Caciocavallo and provola are available at Italian markets or specialty cheese shops.

Red Pepper Soup with Bruschetta

2 servings

4 large red bell peppers
   (1½ pounds total)
5 tablespoons extra-virgin olive oil
¼ cup chicken stock (preferably homemade)
   Salt and freshly ground pepper

1 3 × 2-inch piece Italian bread
   (crust trimmed), cut into six
   ½-inch slices
1 large garlic clove, minced
2 fresh basil leaves

Char peppers over gas flame or in broiler until blackened on all sides. Wrap in paper bag and let stand 20 minutes to steam. Peel, core and seed. Rinse if necessary; pat dry. Puree peppers in processor. With machine running, add 4 tablespoons olive oil and stock through feed tube. Season soup with salt and freshly ground pepper.

Preheat oven to 350°F. Arrange bread on baking sheet. Divide garlic among slices. Drizzle with remaining 1 tablespoon olive oil. Sprinkle with salt. Bake 4 minutes. Transfer bruschettas to broiler and brown, about 1 minute.

Ladle soup into wide shallow bowls. Arrange 3 bruschettas in each. Top with basil. Serve at room temperature.

Chick-Pea, Tomato and Mint Soup

6 servings

1 cup dried chick-peas (garbanzo beans)

1 tablespoon olive oil
1 cup chopped onion
2 teaspoons minced garlic
2 cups chicken stock (preferably homemade)
¾ teaspoon salt
1 1-pound can tomatoes, undrained and coarsely chopped
1 pound fresh tomatoes, peeled and coarsely chopped

3 fresh mint stalks or ¾ teaspoon dried, crumbled
3 2 × 1-inch strips orange peel
¼ teaspoon sugar

¼ cup minced fresh parsley (preferably Italian)
¼ teaspoon freshly ground pepper
   Chopped fresh mint leaves or dried, crumbled

Soak chick-peas overnight in water to cover by at least 1 inch.

Heat oil in heavy large saucepan over medium-high heat. Add ¼ cup onion and 1 teaspoon garlic and stir 3 minutes. Drain chick-peas and add to pan. Add stock and bring to boil. Cover, reduce heat and simmer 30 minutes. Add

½ teaspoon salt and cook 30 minutes longer. Add canned and fresh tomatoes, mint stalks, orange and sugar. Stir in remaining ¾ cup onion, 1 teaspoon garlic and ¼ teaspoon salt. Cover and simmer until chick-peas are tender, stirring occasionally, about 2 hours. Discard mint stalks and orange. (*Can be prepared 1 day ahead and refrigerated. Reheat before continuing.*)

Just before serving, add parsley, pepper and chopped mint. Adjust seasoning.

Lentil Soup with Red Wine

Makes 6 quarts

1 cup minced bacon or blanched salt pork
2 cups minced onion
1 cup grated carrot
1 cup diced celery
½ cup minced fresh parsley
4 garlic cloves, minced
16 cups beef stock
4 cups dried brown or red lentils
4 cups tomato juice
1½ cups dry red wine

Bouquet garni (6 whole cloves, 6 black peppercorns, 2 to 3 inches dried orange peel, 2 bay leaves and 1 thyme sprig wrapped in cheesecloth)

¼ cup fresh lemon juice
Salt and freshly ground pepper
Sour cream
Snipped fresh chives or minced green onion tops

Sauté bacon in 8-quart stockpot over medium heat 2 minutes. Add onion, carrot, celery, parsley and garlic and sauté until bacon is lightly browned, about 10 minutes. Add stock, lentils, tomato juice, wine and bouquet garni. Bring to boil. Reduce heat, cover and simmer until lentils are tender, stirring occasionally, 30 to 35 minutes.

Discard bouquet garni. Coarsely puree soup in blender or processor. Return to pot. Add lemon juice. Season with salt and pepper. Serve hot, garnished with sour cream and chives. (*Can be prepared two days ahead, cooled, covered and refrigerated. Reheat before serving.*)

Tuscan Bean Soup

6 servings

1 pound dried white beans
4 cups water

½ cup olive oil
1 small onion, chopped
1 medium celery stalk, chopped

2 medium garlic cloves, minced
½ pound red cabbage, chopped

½ pound beet greens or Swiss chard, stemmed and chopped
2 medium carrots, peeled and thinly sliced
⅓ cup tomato paste
Salt and freshly ground pepper
6 slices Italian bread, toasted

Combine beans and water in large saucepan and soak overnight.

Simmer beans in soaking water until tender, adding more water if necessary to keep beans covered, about 1 hour.

Heat oil in another heavy large saucepan over low heat. Add onion, celery and garlic. Cook until tender and just golden brown, stirring occasionally, about 15 minutes. Add cabbage and greens and cook until wilted, stirring occasionally, about 5 minutes. Mix in carrots and tomato paste. Puree beans with cooking liquid in processor or blender. Add to vegetables. Cover partially and simmer 40 minutes, thinning with water if desired. Season with salt and pepper. Place toast in bowls. Ladle soup over and serve.

Pasta e Fagioli with Ham, Mushrooms and Herbs

If time permits, cook dried cranberry beans or kidney beans to replace the canned for this version of the Italian peasant classic.

6 servings

2 tablespoons olive oil
2 medium onions, thickly sliced
2 small carrots, thickly sliced
1/2 medium red bell pepper, cut into thin strips
8 ounces smoked ham, cut into 1/4-inch dice (about 1 1/3 cups)
3 tablespoons shredded fresh basil or 1/2 teaspoon dried, crumbled
4 garlic cloves, minced
Pinch of dried oregano, crumbled
1 15 1/4-ounce can tomatoes, drained
6 cups chicken stock, degreased

2 1-pound cans kidney beans, drained and rinsed
2 1/2 cups small pasta such as shells or wheels (rotelle)
Salt and freshly ground pepper
3/4 cup sliced mushrooms
5 tablespoons shredded fresh basil
1/3 cup sliced green onion tops
Olive oil
Freshly grated Parmesan cheese

Heat 2 tablespoons oil in heavy large saucepan over medium heat. Add onions, carrots and bell pepper. Cook until beginning to soften, stirring occasionally, about 8 minutes. Add ham, 3 tablespoons fresh basil, garlic and oregano. Stir 2 minutes. Add tomatoes. Cook until mixture is reduced to thick sauce, crushing tomatoes with spoon, about 6 minutes. Add stock and beans. Bring to boil, mashing 1/4 of beans against sides of pot and skimming surface occasionally. Reduce heat, cover and simmer 15 minutes. (*Can be prepared 1 day ahead*).

Degrease soup. Bring to boil, stirring occasionally. Add pasta. Boil gently until pasta is almost tender but firm to bite, 6 to 7 minutes. Season with salt and pepper. Sprinkle mushrooms over soup. Remove from heat, cover and let stand 5 minutes. Return soup to boil, stirring constantly. Adjust seasoning. Stir in 5 tablespoons fresh basil. Ladle soup into bowls. Top with green onion and drizzle with oil. Pass Parmesan and freshly ground pepper separately.

Bread Soup with Tomatoes

4 to 5 servings

1/4 cup olive oil
1 large onion, sliced
2 to 2 1/2 cups peeled and coarsely chopped tomatoes
2 tablespoons tomato paste

7 cups (or more) water
1/2 pound (about) stale Italian Country Bread (see page 45) or French bread, broken into small chunks

3 to 4 tablespoons chopped fresh basil leaves
3 large garlic cloves, chopped
2 teaspoons salt
Freshly ground pepper
Olive oil

4 to 5 basil leaves (garnish)

Heat 1/4 cup olive oil in heavy 10-inch skillet over medium heat. Add onion and cook until golden but not brown, about 8 minutes. Stir in chopped tomatoes and tomato paste. Reduce heat to low and simmer gently about 20 minutes, stirring occasionally.

Meanwhile, combine 7 cups water with bread in large saucepan. Place over medium heat and cook, stirring, until mixture is smooth and very thick, reducing heat to low and adding more water as necessary. Blend in chopped basil, garlic, salt and pepper and cook about 3 minutes. Stir in tomato mixture. Ladle soup into deep bowls. Drizzle olive oil over top. Garnish with fresh basil leaf.

3 ❧ *Pasta, Grains and Breads*

For originality and creativity, there is nothing quite like Italy's vast repertoire of pasta dishes. Pasta, reduced to its simplest terms, refers to a paste made of flour, water and salt. Often eggs, oil or vegetable purees are added. Gastronomic historians trace its origins to the ancient Romans living in Sicily, and, in fact, the south is where the commercial pasta industry was born in the eighteenth century.

There are countless varieties of pasta; one firm alone lists 52. And many of them are represented in our recipes, such as Fettuccine with Olives and Toasted Pine Nuts (page 24), Fusilli with Eggplant, Prosciutto and Cream (page 24), Pumpkin Turkey Anolini with Sage Butter (page 29) and Linguine with Fresh Tomato Sauce (page 22).

Gnocchi (pronounced nyō-key) are dumplings made from potatoes, farina, semolina or flour, and are often served in place of pasta. Their uninspired look helps explain their literal meaning, "dullard or puddinghead." A few of our never-dull recipes are Potato Gnocchi with Tomato-Porcini Sauce (page 35) and Spinach and Pea Gnocchi (page 36).

Italy is Europe's leading rice producer and, not coincidentally, the most skilled at cooking it. Their most famous rice dish, risotto, is often served instead of pasta. The pearly, short-grained rice called Arborio, from the Po River Valley in the Piedmont region, is ideally suited to this slow-cooked specialty. Our recipes using it include Golden Carrot Risotto (page 41), and Risotto with Shrimp, Mussels and Peas (page 42).

Polenta, cooked cornmeal or maize flour, is one of the staple foods of Northern Italy. In the Friuli region, on the Austrian border, polenta is so popular that it is dipped in milk and eaten for breakfast. In both Friuli and Veneto, grilled or broiled slices of polenta accompany the main course in place of bread. In this collection we show it off in Sweet Polenta with Ricotta (page 40) and Spinach and Polenta Custards (page 40).

Although polenta may sometimes take the place of bread with the main course, in some areas it is rare to find an Italian meal served without a freshly baked loaf of bread on the table. We offer a variety of recipes from which to choose for this ubiquitous accompaniment, from the classic Italian Country Bread (page 45) and Grilled Garlic Bread (page 48) to the heartier Ricotta Cheese Bread (page 47).

 *Pasta*

Linguine with Fresh Tomato Sauce

6 servings

4 tablespoons olive oil
2 tablespoons minced garlic
3 pounds very ripe tomatoes, coarsely chopped, liquid reserved
½ cup coarsely chopped fresh basil
3 tablespoons red wine vinegar
Salt and freshly ground pepper

1 pound linguine
1 tablespoon extra-virgin olive oil
Freshly grated Parmesan cheese

Heat 1 tablespoon oil in heavy small skillet over medium-low heat. Add garlic and stir 3 minutes; do not brown. Transfer to large nonaluminum bowl. Mix in tomatoes and liquid, remaining 3 tablespoons oil, basil and vinegar. Season with salt and pepper. Let stand 6 hours.

Just before serving, cook linguine in large amount of boiling salted water until just tender but still firm to bite. Drain well; transfer to large bowl. Add olive oil and toss well. Add sauce and toss again. Pass Parmesan cheese.

Linguine with Paprika Sauce

An easy-to-make first course.

4 servings

½ cup olive oil
4 garlic cloves, crushed
¼ cup Hungarian sweet paprika
½ cup dry white wine
4 medium tomatoes, peeled and seeded or ¾ cup well-drained canned Italian plum tomatoes
½ teaspoon salt

1 pound linguine
2 tablespoons olive oil
1½ cups (¼ pound) freshly grated Romano cheese
Additional freshly grated Romano cheese

Heat ½ cup oil in heavy 10-inch skillet over low heat. Add garlic and cook until golden brown, about 10 minutes. Discard garlic, using slotted spoon. Add paprika to skillet and stir 5 minutes. Add wine. Increase heat and boil until reduced by half. Finely chop tomatoes in processor or blender. Add to skillet. Stir in salt. Simmer until sauce thickens, about 10 minutes.

Meanwhile, cook linguine in large pot of rapidly boiling salted water until just tender but firm to bite. Drain. Place 2 tablespoons oil on heated platter and add pasta. Spoon sauce over top. Sprinkle with 1½ cups cheese and toss to blend. Serve immediately. Pass additional cheese separately.

Herb Pasta with Double Tomato Sauce

2 servings

1 egg
2 tablespoons chopped fresh parsley
1 tablespoon chopped fresh oregano or 1 teaspoon dried, crumbled
1 tablespoon chopped fresh thyme or 1 teaspoon dried, crumbled
1 cup all purpose flour
1 tablespoon olive oil

¾ teaspoon salt
2 teaspoons (about) water

3 tablespoons freshly grated Parmesan cheese
2 tablespoons (¼ stick) butter, melted
Double Tomato Sauce*

Combine egg and herbs in processor and blend using on/off turns until herbs are minced and completely combined with egg. Add flour, oil and salt and blend well. Add water 1 teaspoon at a time and process until dough forms ball, using only enough water for dough to hold together.

Remove dough from work bowl and flour lightly. Run through pasta machine with rollers at widest setting. Fold dough in half, flour again and repeat rolling. Run through rollers at progressively narrower settings until pasta is desired thickness. Let dry on kitchen towels until firm but not brittle. Cut into noodles about ¼ inch wide. (*Herb pasta can be prepared ahead to this point and dried and frozen.*)

Bring large pot of salted water to rapid boil over high heat. Add pasta and cover pot just until water returns to boil. Uncover and boil until pasta is al dente, about 1 to 2 minutes. Drain in colander. Transfer to bowl. Add cheese and melted butter and toss gently. Divide between heated plates. Spoon on sauce and serve.

*Double Tomato Sauce

Makes ½ to ¾ cup

2 tablespoons olive oil
1 tablespoon butter
½ medium onion (about 2½ ounces), finely chopped
1 large tomato, peeled, seeded and chopped

1 tablespoon tomato paste
1 ounce sun-dried tomatoes (optional), patted dry and minced

Heat oil and butter in heavy medium skillet over low heat. Add onion and cook until translucent and very tender, about 15 minutes. Add chopped tomato and tomato paste. Increase heat to medium and cook until all liquid is absorbed and tomato is soft, about 20 mintues. Stir in minced dried tomatoes and serve.

Fettuccine with Olives and Toasted Pine Nuts

6 servings

¾ cup freshly grated Parmesan cheese (2 ounces)
3 eggs
1 pound fresh fettuccine
½ cup finely chopped brine-cured olives (such as Gaeta*)

½ cup pine nuts, toasted
¼ teaspoon freshly grated nutmeg
Salt and freshly ground pepper

Whisk Parmesan and eggs in large bowl. Cook fettuccine in large pot of boiling salted water until tender but still firm to bite. Drain. Toss with Parmesan mixture. Sprinkle with olives, pine nuts, nutmeg, salt and pepper; toss again. Serve immediately.

*Available at Italian markets.

Fusilli with Vodka

6 first-course or 4 main-course servings

1 small dried red chili, halved
¾ cup vodka

2⅔ cups whipping cream
10 tablespoons (1¼ sticks) unsalted butter
6 ounces tomatoes, peeled, seeded and chopped

1 pound fusilli (corkscrew pasta)
¾ cup freshly grated Parmesan cheese (3 ounces)
3 tablespoons minced fresh parsley
Additional freshly grated Parmesan cheese
Freshly ground pepper

Soak chili in vodka 24 hours.

Combine cream, butter and tomatoes in heavy large saucepan. Simmer until reduced by ⅓, about 12 minutes.

Add pasta to large amount of rapidly boiling salted water, stirring to prevent sticking. Cook until just tender but still firm to bite. Drain well. Add to sauce. Boil 1 minute, stirring constantly. Discard chili; add vodka to pasta. Simmer until sauce thickens, stirring constantly, about 3 minutes. Mix in ¾ cup Parmesan and parsley. Serve immediately, passing additional Parmesan and pepper separately.

Fusilli with Eggplant, Prosciutto and Cream

2 to 4 servings

1 large eggplant, unpeeled, cut into ¾-inch dice
½ teaspoon salt
2 large garlic cloves
1 large red onion, peeled and halved lengthwise
2 tablespoons (¼ stick) unsalted butter
¾ cup whipping cream
3 ounces prosciutto, cut into fine julienne

¾ teaspoon freshly grated nutmeg
Salt and freshly ground pepper

6 ounces (about 3 cups) freshly cooked fusilli or tubular pasta
2 tablespoons (¼ stick) unsalted butter, cut into 4 pieces, room temperature
Minced or shredded Parmesan or Romano cheese (preferably imported)

Place eggplant in colander. Sprinkle with ½ teaspoon salt. Let stand 45 to 60 minutes. Rinse under cold water. Drain eggplant thoroughly.

Drop garlic through processor feed tube and, with machine running, mince. Leave garlic in work bowl.

Stand onion in feed tube and cut with french fry disc using firm pressure. Melt 2 tablespoons butter in heavy 12-inch skillet over medium-high heat. Add onion and garlic and cook until soft, stirring frequently, about 3 minutes. Stir in eggplant and cream. Reduce heat to medium, cover and cook until eggplant is tender, 7 to 8 minutes. Remove from heat. Mix in prosciutto and nutmeg. Season with salt and pepper. (*Can be prepared 3 days ahead and refrigerated. Rewarm over low heat.*)

Toss fusilli with 2 tablespoons butter in large bowl. Add sauce and toss well. Divide among plates. Sprinkle with Parmesan. Serve immediately, passing remaining Parmesan separately.

Farfalle with Leeks, Celery and Walnuts

2 to 4 servings

½ cup walnuts

2 large leeks, white and light green parts only, cut into feed-tube lengths

3 medium celery stalks, strings removed, cut into feed-tube lengths

1 tablespoon olive oil (preferably extra-virgin)

2 tablespoons (¼ stick) unsalted butter

¼ teaspoon salt

½ cup beef stock

¼ cup dry Marsala

6 anchovies, rinsed and quartered

3 tablespoons well-chilled unsalted butter, cut into 3 pieces

6 ounces (about 3 cups) freshly cooked farfalle (bow tie pasta) Minced or shredded Parmesan or Romano cheese (preferably imported)

Place walnuts in food processor work bowl and coarsely chop using on/off turns. Remove from bowl.

Insert thick slicer. Stand leeks and celery in feed tube and slice using medium pressure. Heat oil in heavy 10-inch skillet over medium heat. Add walnuts and cook until golden, stirring frequently, about 4 minutes. Remove walnuts; set aside. Melt 2 tablespoons butter in same skillet over medium heat. Add leek mixture and salt and cook until vegetables begin to soften, stirring frequently, about 5 minutes. Stir in stock, Marsala and anchovies. Continue cooking until vegetables are just crisp-tender, stirring frequently, about 5 minutes. Stir in 3 tablespoons butter 1 piece at a time, incorporating each piece completely before adding next. Taste and adjust seasoning.

Toss pasta with sauce in large bowl. Mix in reserved walnuts. Divide among plates. Sprinkle with Parmesan. Serve immediately, passing remaining Parmesan separately.

Hay and Straw Fettuccine with Red Pepper and Mushroom Sauce

A lusty pasta course based on a classic dish. Remaining cut fettuccine can be frozen and used at another time.

8 servings

Hay Fettuccine
- 6 cups loosely packed watercress leaves (2 bunches)
- 2 cups (or more) all purpose flour
- 2 eggs
- ½ teaspoon salt

Straw Fettuccine
- 1½ cups all purpose flour
- 2 eggs
- 1 tablespoon curry powder
- ½ teaspoon salt

Sauce
- ½ cup (1 stick) butter
- 3 garlic cloves, minced
- 2 red bell peppers, cut into 1 × ¼-inch strips
- 1 pound mushrooms, sliced
- ½ cup beef stock
- ¾ cup whipping cream
  Salt

Freshly grated Parmesan cheese

For hay: Puree watercress in processor. Add 2 cups flour, eggs and salt. Process until ball forms. Wrap in plastic and let rest at least 30 minutes.

For straw: Blend all ingredients in processor until ball forms. Wrap in plastic and let rest at least 30 minutes.

Cut hay pasta dough into 4 pieces. Flatten 1 piece of dough (keep remainder covered), then fold in thirds and dust with flour. Turn pasta machine to widest setting and run dough through until smooth and velvety, folding before each run and flouring as necessary. Adjust pasta machine to next narrower setting. Run dough through machine without folding. Repeat, narrowing rollers after each run, until pasta is ¹⁄₁₆ inch thick, dusting with flour as necessary. Hang dough sheet on rack or place on towels. Repeat with remaining hay pasta dough.

Repeat process with straw pasta dough.

Set all pasta aside until sheets look leathery and edges begin to curl, 10 to 30 minutes, depending on dampness of dough. *Pasta must be cut at this point or dough will be too brittle.*

Run dough sheets through fettuccine blades of pasta machine. Arrange strands on kitchen towel, overlapping as little as possible, until ready to cook. (*Pasta can be frozen 3 months.*)

For sauce: Melt butter in heavy large skillet over medium-low heat. Add garlic and stir 1 minute. Add peppers and cook until beginning to soften, stirring frequently, about 5 minutes. Add mushrooms and cook until soft, stirring frequently, about 4 minutes. Mix in broth. Simmer 20 minutes to blend flavors. (*Can be prepared 1 day ahead and refrigerated.*)

Add cream to sauce and simmer until slightly thickened, about 5 minutes. Season to taste with salt.

Meanwhile, add ½ pound hay pasta and ½ pound straw pasta to large pot of rapidly boiling salted water, stirring to prevent sticking. Cook until just tender but still firm to bite, about 30 seconds. Drain. Toss with sauce. Divide among plates. Top with Parmesan cheese and serve immediately.

Whole Wheat Fettuccine with Country Ham and Watercress

4 to 6 servings

¼ cup (½ stick) unsalted butter
4 ounces country ham, cut into
  ¼-inch dice

1½ cups whipping cream
  Pinch of freshly grated nutmeg

1 cup freshly grated Parmesan
  cheese

Whole Wheat Fettuccine*
3 large bunches watercress, tough
  stems removed (about 8 cups)
Salt and freshly ground pepper

Melt butter in heavy small saucepan over medium heat. Add ham and cook until crisp and lightly browned, stirring occasionally, 10 to 15 minutes.

Pour off fat from pan. Stir in cream and nutmeg and bring to boil. Reduce heat and simmer until reduced by ⅓, about 15 minutes. Remove from heat. Stir in ¼ cup Parmesan. Keep warm.

Cook fettuccine in large pot of boiling salted water until just tender but still firm to bite. Drain; return immediately to pot. Add sauce and watercress and bring to simmer. Toss 1 minute. Season with salt and pepper. Divide among plates. Serve immediately. Pass additional Parmesan separately.

*Whole Wheat Fettuccine

4 to 6 servings

3 eggs, room temperature
3 tablespoons olive oil
  Pinch of salt

1 cup whole wheat flour, preferably
  stone-ground
1 cup unbleached all purpose flour

Whisk eggs, oil and salt in small bowl. Combine whole wheat flour and ¾ cup unbleached flour in processor using several on/off turns. With machine running, blend in egg mixture through feed tube. Turn dough out onto lightly floured surface. Knead in enough of remaining flour to form smooth dough. Wrap in plastic. Let stand at room temperature 1 hour.

Cut dough in half. Flatten 1 piece (keep other covered), then fold in thirds. Turn pasta machine to widest setting and run dough through several times until smooth and velvety, folding before each run and dusting with flour if sticky. Adjust machine to next narrower setting. Run dough through machine without folding. Repeat narrowing rollers after each run, until pasta is ¹⁄₁₆ inch thick, dusting with flour as necessary. Hang dough sheet on drying rack or place on kitchen towels. Repeat with remaining dough. Set aside until sheets look leathery and edges begin to curl, 10 to 30 minutes, depending on dampness of dough. *Pasta must be cut at this point or dough will be too brittle.* Run sheets through fettuccine blades of pasta machine (*or cut by hand into ¼-inch-wide strips*). Arrange pasta on towel, overlapping as little as possible until ready to cook.

Brigands' Pasta

14 servings

2¾ pounds broccoli, trimmed
1 cup olive oil
5 large garlic cloves, flattened
   and peeled
4 pounds tomatoes, peeled, seeded
   and coarsely chopped
   Salt

1 cup raisins
1 cup pine nuts

1 pound penne or other short
   tubular pasta
1 pound rotelle or fusilli pasta
1 cup loosely packed whole Italian
   parsley leaves

Cut broccoli florets into 1 × ½-inch pieces. Peel broccoli stems and cut into ½-inch pieces. Cook broccoli in large pan of boiling salted water until just tender, 5 to 7 minutes. Drain; plunge in ice water to cool. Drain and pat dry.

Combine oil and garlic in heavy large skillet over low heat. Cook until garlic is golden brown, about 4 minutes. Discard garlic. Add tomatoes and salt to skillet, increase heat to medium-low and cook 10 minutes, stirring occasionally. Add raisins and pine nuts and cook 5 minutes, stirring occasionally. Add raisins and pine nuts and cook 5 minutes. Add broccoli and mix until heated through.

Meanwhile, cook penne and rotelle in separate large saucepans of boiling salted water until just tender but firm to bite. Drain well. Combine in large heated bowl. Mix in sauce and parsley. Serve pasta immediately.

Pasta with Creamy Ricotta Pesto

6 to 8 servings

¾ cup fresh basil
¼ cup fresh parsley
1 garlic clove
¼ cup olive oil
1 cup ricotta cheese
1 pound fettuccine, freshly cooked

1 pint cherry tomatoes, stemmed
   and halved
   Freshly grated Parmesan or
   Romano cheese

Mince basil, parsley and garlic in food processor or blender. Add oil and process until thick, about 10 seconds. Add ricotta and process until well blended. Arrange pasta on serving platter. Pour pesto over and toss to coat well. Top with tomatoes. Serve immediately, passing grated cheese separately.

Three-Cheese Ravioli with Sage Butter Sauce

These can be made ahead and frozen.

8 servings

Pasta
2¼ to 2½ cups all purpose flour
½ teaspoon salt
3 eggs
1 tablespoon water
1 teaspoon olive oil

Filling
½ pound fresh ricotta cheese
¼ pound fresh mozzarella cheese,
   finely diced
¼ cup freshly grated Parmesan
   cheese (preferably imported)

Sauce
6 tablespoons (¾ stick) butter
35 small fresh sage leaves
   Salt and freshly ground pepper

2 tablespoons vegetable oil
   Freshly grated Parmesan cheese
   (preferably imported)

For pasta: Sift 2¼ cups flour and salt onto work surface. Form into mound and make well in center. Add eggs, water and oil to well; blend with fork. Gradually draw flour from inner edge of well into center until all flour is incorporated. Clean hands and work surface. Knead dough until soft and pliable, adding more flour if sticky, about 8 minutes. (*Dough can also be made in processor.*) Wrap in plastic bag and let stand 30 minutes.

For filling: Using electric mixer, beat ricotta until smooth. Mix in cheeses.

Cut pasta dough into 8 pieces. Flatten 1 piece (keep remainder wrapped in plastic bag), then fold in thirds. Turn pasta machine to widest setting and run dough through several times until smooth and velvety, folding before each run and dusting with flour if sticky. Adjust machine to next narrower setting. Run dough through machine without folding. Repeat, narrowing rollers after each run until pasta sheet is ¹/₁₆ inch thick, dusting with flour as necessary.

Arrange dough sheet on work surface. Spoon filling onto dough by teaspoonfuls, spacing 1½ inches apart and 1 inch in from edges. Roll second sheet of dough as above. Brush water on first sheet between and around filling. Top with second sheet of dough. Press between filling to seal pasta. Cut ravioli into squares, using pasta cutter-sealer. (*Can also be formed in ravioli tray.*) Transfer ravioli to floured towel, spacing slightly. Repeat with remaining pasta and filling. (*Can be prepared 1 day ahead, covered with floured towel and refrigerated or 1 month ahead and frozen on baking sheet. Wrap in plastic bag when solid. Do not thaw ravioli before cooking.*)

For sauce: Melt butter in heavy small saucepan over low heat. Add sage, salt and pepper. Keep warm.

Add oil to large pot of boiling salted water. Add pasta and stir gently until water returns to boil. Cook pasta until tender, about 6 minutes. Drain well. Transfer to heated bowl. Mix in sage butter. Sprinkle with Parmesan. Serve immediately, passing additional cheese.

Pumpkin Turkey Anolini with Sage Butter

Leftover cooked turkey can be used in the filling for these savory pasta rounds.

12 servings

Turkey Filling
- 1 cup canned solid pack pumpkin
- ¼ cup (½ stick) unsalted butter
- 1 pound boned turkey breast, cut into 2-inch-thick slices
- 6 fresh sage leaves of ¼ teaspoon dried, crumbled
  Salt and freshly ground pepper

- ¾ cup freshly grated Parmesan cheese (preferably imported)
- 2 egg yolks
- 1 egg
- 3 tablespoons amaretto liqueur
- 2 teaspoons orange marmalade
- ¼ teaspoon freshly grated nutmeg

Pasta Dough
- 3 eggs
- 2 tablespoons plus 1 teaspoon water
- 1 teaspoon olive oil
  Pinch of salt
- 1½ cups (or more) all purpose flour
- ½ cup semolina flour or all purpose flour

  Sage Butter*
  Freshly grated Parmesan cheese
  Freshly ground pepper
  Sage leaves

For filling: Preheat oven to 350°F. Bake pumpkin in pie plate 30 minutes, stirring occasionally. Cool. Melt butter in heavy large skillet over medium-low heat. Add turkey and sage. Sprinkle with salt and pepper. Cook just until turkey is springy to touch, about 10 minutes per side. Cool 15 minutes.

Cut turkey into 1-inch pieces. Place in processor with cooking juices. Chop medium-fine, using on/off turns. Transfer to large bowl. Mix in ²/₃ cup pumpkin, Parmesan, yolks, egg, amaretto, marmalade and nutmeg. Season with salt and pepper. (*Can be prepared 1 day ahead and refrigerated.*)

For pasta: Blend eggs, water, oil and salt in processor. Add 1½ cups all purpose flour and semolina flour. Process just until ball forms, adding more all purpose flour if necessary. Dust dough with flour. Place in bowl, cover with plastic and let stand 30 minutes.

Cut dough into 8 pieces. Flatten 1 piece (keep remainder covered to prevent drying), then fold into thirds. Turn pasta machine to widest setting and run dough through several times until smooth and velvety, folding before each run and dusting with flour if sticky. Adjust machine to next narrower setting. Run dough through machine without folding. Repeat, narrowing rollers after each run until pasta forms ¹/₁₆-inch-thick 2-inch-wide strip, dusting with flour as necessary.

Arrange dough sheet on floured surface. Place teaspoons of filling down center of half the length of dough spacing 2 inches apart. Fold remaining half of dough over. Press dough down between filling. Using cookie cutter, cut around filling into 2-inch rounds. Crimp edges with tines of fork to seal. Dust anolini with flour and place on floured towel, leaving spaces between. Repeat with remaining dough and filling. Let anolini dry 1 hour. (*Can be prepared 1 day ahead. Cover with floured towel and refrigerate.*)

Shake flour from anolini. Add anolini to large pot of rapidly boiling salted water, stirring to prevent sticking. Cook until just tender, about 7 minutes. Drain. Turn onto heated platter. Pour Sage Butter over and stir gently to coat. Sprinkle generously with Parmesan and pepper. Garnish with sage.

* Sage Butter

Makes about 1½ cups

1½ cups (3 sticks) butter	Salt
14 fresh sage leaves, minced or ³/₄ teaspoon dried, crumbled	

Heat butter with sage in heavy small saucepan over low heat until butter melts and is light golden brown, stirring occasionally. Season with salt.

Cannelloni alla Nizzarda

4 main-course or 6 first-course servings

4 dried mushrooms, preferably porcini	3 tablespoons butter, chopped, room temperature
1¼ cups hot water	2 tablespoons freshly grated Parmesan cheese
2 tablespoons (¼ stick) butter	Salt and freshly ground pepper
1 medium-large onion, minced	
1 large carrot, minced	Butter
1 medium celery stalk, minced	16 Italian Crepes*
1 pound ground veal	2 cups Salsa Balsamella**
1 cup dry white wine	3 tablespoons freshly grated Parmesan cheese
²/₃ cup whipping cream or milk	
2 cups veal or chicken stock	

Soak mushrooms in hot water 30 minutes. Drain, rinse and squeeze dry. Reserve soaking liquid. Discard hard stems; mince mushrooms finely. Strain liquid through fine sieve lined with dampened paper towel and set aside.

Melt 2 tablespoons butter in heavy large saucepan over low heat. Add onion, carrot and celery. Cover and cook 10 minutes, stirring occasionally. Increase heat to medium. Add veal and cook until veal turns pink, crumbling with fork, about 5 minutes. Stir in minced mushrooms and wine. Boil until liquid is reduced to 3 tablespoons, about 6 minutes. Pour in cream and boil until liquid is reduced to 3 tablespoons, about 8 minutes. Blend in soaking liquid and veal stock and bring to boil. Reduce heat to low, cover partially and simmer gently until all liquid is absorbed, stirring occasionally, about 3 hours.

Whisk 3 tablespoons butter into veal mixture. Stir in 2 tablespoons Parmesan. Season with salt and pepper. (*Can be prepared several days ahead, covered with plastic and refrigerated.*)

Preheated oven to 425°F. Butter large gratin pan. Spread second-cooked side of each crepe with about 1¾ tablespoons veal. Roll crepes up to form cylinders. Arrange seam side down in prepared pans. Spoon Salsa Balsamella over. Sprinkle with 3 tablespoons Parmesan. (*Can be prepared 1 day ahead to this point, covered with plastic and refrigerated. Bring to room temperature before baking.*) Bake until cheese is melted and browned and sauce is bubbling, about 15 minutes. Serve immediately.

*Italian Crepes

Makes about sixteen 7-inch crepes

1 cup all purpose flour	Pinch of freshly ground pepper
2 eggs	Pinch of freshly grated nutmeg
1 egg yolk	
1 cup milk	3 tablespoons butter
½ teaspoon salt	Milk (if necessary)

Make well in center of flour in large bowl. Add eggs and yolk to well and whisk to blend. Gradually incorporate flour, whisking until mixture is smooth. Whisk in milk in slow steady stream until smooth. Season with salt, pepper and nutmeg. Let batter stand 1 hour at room temperature. (*Can be prepared 1 day ahead to this point, covered with plastic and refrigerated. Bring to room temperature before continuing.*)

Melt butter in 7-inch crepe pan or heavy skillet. Cool slightly. Stir half into batter. Pour remaining butter into small cup. Skim off foam to clarify.

Heat crepe pan over medium-high heat. Brush lightly with clarified butter. Remove pan from heat. Stir batter and ladle about 3 tablespoons into corner of pan, tilting so batter just coats bottom. Return excess to bowl. Cook crepe until bottom is brown, loosening edges with tip of small knife. Turn or flip crepe and cook until second side is speckled brown. Slide out onto plate. Repeat with remaining batter, stirring often. (Thin batter with milk if too thick.) Adjust heat and add clarified butter to pan as necessary. (*Crepes can be prepared up to 4 days ahead, wrapped tightly in plastic and refrigerated, or frozen several months when overwrapped in freezer paper.*)

**Salsa Balsamella

Makes 2 cups

3 tablespoons butter	3 tablespoons freshly grated Parmesan cheese
1 large shallot or ½ small onion, minced	3 to 4 tablespoons whipping cream
3 tablespoons all purpose flour	⅛ teaspoon freshly grated nutmeg
2 cups milk	Salt and freshly ground pepper

Melt butter in heavy small saucepan over low heat. Add shallot and stir until translucent, about 3 minutes. Add flour and stir 3 minutes. Stir in milk. Increase heat to medium-high and bring to boil, whisking constantly. Reduce heat and simmer 10 minutes, stirring occasionally. Strain through fine sieve. Blend in cheese. Add enough cream to make medium-thick sauce. Season with nutmeg, salt and pepper.

Candy-shaped-Pasta Pie

Two delicious sauces accent the filling in this classic recipe. If time is at a premium, store-bought stuffed tortellini can be used instead of the homemade caramelle pasta. Or, you could make only the stuffed pasta and serve it with one or both of the sauces.

8 servings

Pastry
- 2 cups all purpose flour
- 1 tablespoon sugar
- ½ teaspoon salt
- 6 tablespoons (¾ stick) well-chilled butter, diced
- 1 egg, chilled
- 1 egg yolk, chilled
- ½ cup (about) ice water

Pasta
- 2 eggs, room temperature
- 2 teaspoons olive oil
- 1½ cups all purpose flour
- ½ teaspoon salt

Filling
- 2 teaspoons butter
- 1 teaspoon vegetable oil
- ¼ pound lean pork loin, cut into 1-inch cubes
- ¼ pound chicken breast, skinned, boned and cut into 1-inch pieces
- 3 ounces mortadella
- ⅓ cup freshly grated Parmesan cheese
- 1 egg, beaten to blend

Salt and freshly ground pepper
Freshly grated nutmeg

- 1 egg beaten with 1 teaspoon water (glaze)

Porcini-Tomato Sauce
- 1 ounce dried porcini mushrooms
- 2 tablespoons (¼ stick) butter
- 2 tablespoons minced onion
- 2 tablespoons minced carrot
- 1 tablespoon minced celery
- 1½ cups chopped canned Italian plum tomatoes, with liquid
  Salt and freshly ground pepper

Béchamel
- ¼ cup (½ stick) butter
- 3 tablespoons all purpose flour
- 2¼ cups milk, heated
  Salt and freshly ground pepper
  Freshly grated nutmeg
- ½ cup (2 ounces) freshly grated Parmesan cheese

- 1 tablespoon salt
- 1 tablespoon olive oil

For pastry: Combine flour, sugar and salt in processor. Cut in butter using on/off turns until mixture resembles coarse meal. Whisk together egg and yolk. Blend into flour mixture. With machine running, add water through feed tube 1 tablespoon at a time until dough holds together. (*Can also be made by hand.*) Turn dough out onto surface. Knead briefly to form smooth dough. Wrap in floured waxed paper. Refrigerate at least 30 minutes.

Grease 9-inch springform pan. Roll ⅔ of dough out on lightly floured surface to ⅛-inch-thick round. Wrap remaining dough. Fit dough into prepared pan. Refrigerate pan and remaining dough until ready to use. (*Can be prepared 3 days ahead and refrigerated or 1 month ahead and frozen.*)

For pasta: Blend eggs and oil in processor. Add ½ cup flour and salt and mix until thick and smooth. With machine running, gradually add remaining flour through feed tube and blend until soft and smooth; dough should not be sticky. Knead 45 seconds. (*Can also be made by hand.*) Turn dough out onto lightly floured surface. Cover with bowl. Let stand 30 minutes.

For filling: Melt butter with oil in heavy medium skillet over medium heat. Add pork and brown well on all sides. Add chicken and cook until no pink remains, stirring frequently, 5 to 7 minutes. Transfer to processor. Add mortadella. Chop finely using on/off turns; do not puree. Blend in cheese, egg, salt, pepper and nutmeg. (*Can be prepared 2 days ahead and refrigerated.*)

To assemble: Cut pasta dough into egg-size pieces. Flatten 1 piece of dough (keep remainder covered), then fold in thirds. Turn pasta machine to widest setting and run dough through several times until smooth and velvety, folding before each run and dusting with flour if sticky. Adjust machine to next narrower setting. Run dough through machine without folding. Repeat narrowing rollers after each run until pasta is thickness of dime and sheet measures about 4½ × 32 inches.

Trim ends with fluted pastry wheel; reserve scraps. Mound 1 teaspoon filling 1 inch in from short end. Repeat 7 times at 1-inch intervals down center of sheet. Brush between filling and along edges with glaze. Fold dough over filling; press edges to seal. Using fluted pastry cutter, cut along edges and between filling to separate. Pinch dough together on both sides of filling so pasta resembles cellophane-wrapped candy. Set on floured kitchen towel. Repeat with remaining dough and filling. (*Can be prepared 4 hours ahead, covered and stored at room temperature, 1 day ahead and refrigerated or 1 month ahead and frozen. To freeze, place pasta on baking sheet in freezer until hardened. Transfer to storage container.*)

For sauce: Soak porcini in warm water to cover 30 minutes. Drain, reserving liquid. Rinse mushrooms; squeeze dry. Chop into small pieces. Strain soaking liquid through sieve lined with several layers of dampened cheesecloth; reserve ½ cup soaking liquid.

Melt butter in heavy medium saucepan over medium-low heat. Add onion, carrot and celery and cook until softened, stirring occasionally, about 5 minutes. Add porcini and cook 2 minutes. Add soaking liquid, tomatoes, salt and pepper and bring to boil. Reduce heat and simmer gently until sauce is thick enough to mound on spoon, about 45 minutes. (*Can be prepared 4 days ahead and refrigerated.*)

For béchamel: Melt butter in heavy medium saucepan over low heat. Whisk in flour and cook 3 minutes. Whisk in milk, increase heat and bring to boil, stirring constantly. Season with salt, pepper and nutmeg. Reduce heat and simmer until reduced to 1¾ cups, about 20 minutes, stirring occasionally. Mix in cheese. (*Can be prepared 2 days ahead, covered and refrigerated.*)

To cook pasta: Bring large pot of water to boil. Add 1 tablespoon salt and 1 tablespoon oil. Add 8 to 10 pasta pieces and boil 1½ minutes; pasta will be slightly undercooked. Remove using slotted spoon. Refresh in cold water. Set on kitchen towel and dry. Repeat with remaining pasta.

To assemble: Position rack in bottom of oven and preheat to 400°F. Whisk béchamel over medium-low heat until warm. Toss pasta with béchamel. Spread pastry shell with thin layer of tomato sauce. Cover with ⅓ of pasta. Top with ⅓ of remaining tomato sauce. Continue layering with remaining pasta and sauce, ending with sauce. Brush edges of pastry shell with glaze. Roll remaining ⅓ of dough out on lightly floured surface into ⅛-inch-thick round. Drape over pie. Trim and pinch edges. Brush top with glaze. Using fork, pierce top in several places. If desired, gather dough scraps, reroll and cut out decorations. Affix to top of pie. (*Can be prepared 4 hours ahead; store at room temperature.*) Bake pie 20 minutes. Transfer rack and pie to middle of oven and bake until crust is golden brown, 30 to 35 minutes. Cool 10 minutes in pan. Remove springform. Serve immediately.

Scallop-filled Pasta Flowers

6 servings

Fresh Tomato Sauce
2 tablespoons (¼ stick) butter
½ cup minced onion
2 pounds tomatoes, peeled, seeded and chopped or canned Italian plum tomatoes, drained and chopped
1 tablespoon sugar
2 garlic cloves, minced
1 bouquet garni (thyme, parsley sprigs, bay leaf)
1 4-inch strip orange peel

Scallop Filling
¾ pound bay scallops
1 cup milk

¼ cup (½ stick) butter
1 medium onion, chopped
3 bacon slices, chopped
1 garlic clove, minced
3 tablespoons all purpose flour

3 tablespoons dry Sherry
Minced fresh parsley
Fresh lemon juice
Salt and freshly ground pepper

Herb Pasta
1 cup (or more) all purpose flour
¾ teaspoon salt
3 tablespoons olive oil
1 egg
2 tablespoons minced fresh parsley
1 tablespoon minced fresh oregano or 1 teaspoon dried, crumbled
1 tablespoon minced fresh thyme or 1 teaspoon dried, crumbled

2 tablespoons (¼ stick) butter, cut into pieces
Olive oil

For sauce: Melt butter in heavy large skillet over low heat. Add onion, cover and cook until translucent, stirring occasionally, about 10 minutes. Add tomatoes, sugar, garlic, bouquet garni and orange peel. Simmer until thickened, stirring occasionally, about 30 minutes. Puree through food mill or press through fine sieve. (*Can be prepared 2 days ahead. Cool completely. Cover tightly and refrigerate.*)

For filling: Heat scallops and milk in heavy small saucepan just until milk bubbles around edge. Remove from heat and let stand until ready to use.

Melt butter in heavy medium saucepan over medium heat. Add onion, bacon and garlic and cook until mixture is lightly browned, stirring occasionally, about 10 minutes. Reduce heat to low. Stir in flour and cook 3 minutes. Strain milk into saucepan, stirring constantly. Add Sherry and bring to boil. Cook until thickened, stirring constantly, about 5 minutes. Season to taste with parsley, lemon juice, salt and pepper. Cool completely. Stir in scallops.

For pasta: Combine flour and salt. Mound on surface and make well in center. Add 1 tablespoon oil, egg and herbs to well and blend with fork. Gradually draw flour from inner edge of well into center until all flour is incorporated. Gather dough into ball. Wrap in plastic and let rest 30 minutes.

Divide dough in half. Flatten 1 piece (cover remainder to keep from drying), then fold in half or thirds. Turn pasta machine to widest setting and run dough through until smooth and velvety, about 10 times, folding before each run and dusting with flour if necessary. Adjust pasta machine to next narrower setting. Run dough through machine without folding. Repeat, narrowing rollers after each run, until pasta is 1/16 inch thick. Hang dough sheets on drying rack or place on kitchen towels. Repeat with remaining dough. Set aside until sheets look leathery and edges begin to curl. Pasta must be cut at this point or dough will become too brittle to handle.

Cut sheets into 6-inch lengths. Using hands, stretch each to at least 6-inch round. Trim into 6-inch round, using cutter. Cut scraps into strips.

Bring large pot of salted water with remaining 2 tablespoons oil to boil. Add pasta rounds. When rounds float to top, remove using slotted spoon and drain on towel. Add strips and cook until firm but tender to bite. Remove using slotted spoon and drain on towel.

Arrange rounds on surface. Spoon scallop filling into center of each round. Bring up edges and gather in center. Pinch center together; secure with toothpick. Tie pasta strips around top to form flower. (*Can be prepared 1 day ahead. Cover and refrigerate.*)

Preheat oven to 425°F. Bring sauce to boil. Whisk in 2 tablespoons butter 1 piece at a time. Divide sauce among 6 ovenproof dishes. Place pasta flower atop sauce. Brush with olive oil. Bake until heated through and light golden brown, about 10 to 15 minutes. Serve immediately.

Semolina Gnocchi

8 to 10 servings

4½ cups milk
1½ cups plus 6 tablespoons semolina flour*
3 egg yolks, room temperature
¾ cup (1½ sticks) butter
9 tablespoons freshly grated Parmesan cheese

¼ teaspoon freshly grated nutmeg
Salt and freshly ground white pepper

1 tablespoon dry breadcrumbs (optional)

Rinse jelly roll pan under cold water, shaking off excess. Bring milk to boil in heavy large saucepan over medium heat. Gradually whisk in flour and cook 20 minutes, stirring constantly. Remove from heat. Beat in yolks, ¼ cup butter, 3 tablespoons Parmesan and nutmeg. Season with salt and pepper. Spread evenly on prepared sheet. Refrigerate until no longer sticky to touch, about 2 hours.

Preheat oven to 450°F. Cut dough into 2-inch rounds or irregular diamond-shaped strips. Melt remaining butter. Lightly butter 8 × 13-inch ovenproof glass baking dish. Arrange gnocchi in single layer in prepared dish. Drizzle with some of melted butter. Sprinkle with some of Parmesan. Repeat with remaining ingredients, staggering each layer (do not stack gnocchi directly on top of each other). Sprinkle top with breadcrumbs if desired. Bake 20 minutes. Increase oven temperature to 500°F. Bake 5 minutes. Serve gnocchi immediately.

*Available at Italian markets, specialty foods stores and some supermarkets.

Potato Gnocchi with Tomato-Porcini Sauce

8 to 10 servings

6 large baking potatoes (about 4⅛ pounds)
2 eggs
2½ cups (or more) all purpose flour
9 quarts water

3 tablespoons coarse kosher salt
Tomato-Porcini Sauce*
2 tablespoons (¼ stick) butter
Freshly grated Parmesan cheese

Bake potatoes until tender. While hot, cut in half and scoop out pulp. Work pulp through ricer into large bowl (or mash using up-and-down motion only). Using fork, stir in eggs. Blend in ½ cup flour. Turn dough out onto work surface. Gradually knead in 2 cups flour. Continue kneading until smooth and elastic, about 10 minutes. Shape dough into 6 × 4-inch loaf. Cut loaf into 1-inch strips. Roll strips into cylinders ½ inch in diameter. Cut cylinders into 1¼-inch pieces. Boil 1 piece 2 to 3 minutes. If piece falls apart, add more flour to dough ¼ cup at a time until pieces hold together when boiled. Using floured fork, press tines downward into each piece so it curls around fork. Arrange in single layer without touching on generously floured towel. Let gnocchi stand 3 to 4 hours at room temperature to dry.

Bring water and salt to boil. Add gnocchi. Stir gently with wooden spoon. When gnocchi come to surface let cook 2 minutes. Drain well. Place on platter. Spoon sauce over. Dot with butter. Sprinkle with Parmesan.

*Tomato-Porcini Sauce

Makes about 4 cups

1 ounce dried Italian porcini mushrooms	2 large garlic cloves, minced
¼ cup (½ stick) unsalted butter	1 28-ounce can Italian plum tomatoes seeded and coarsely chopped, liquid reserved and strained
¼ cup olive oil	
1 large onion, chopped	⅓ cup tomato paste
1 5-inch celery stalk, chopped	Salt and freshly ground pepper
1 small carrot, chopped	
⅔ cup minced fresh parsley	

Soak porcini in hot water to cover until softened, about 30 minutes. Pour liquid through several layers of dampened cheesecloth. Squeeze porcini dry; chop coarsely, discarding hard core.

Melt butter with oil in heavy large skillet over medium-low heat. Add onion, celery, carrot, parsley and garlic and cook until onion is soft and golden brown, stirring occasionally, about 20 minutes. Add porcini, strained porcini soaking liquid, tomatoes, tomato liquid and paste. Season with salt and pepper. Cover and simmer until sauce is thick, stirring occasionally and adding hot water if necessary, about 1½ hours. Serve immediately. (*Can be prepared several days ahead. Cool completely, cover and refrigerate. Reheat gently before serving.*)

Spinach and Pea Gnocchi

Crisp on the outside and light in the center, these gnocchi make a tempting first course or main dish.

Makes about 50

1 pound ricotta	2 extra-large egg yolks
1 pound fresh spinach, stemmed, or one 10-ounce package frozen whole leaf spinach, thawed	1 extra-large egg
	1½ cups (about) dry breadcrumbs
2 pounds fresh peas, shelled, or one 10-ounce package frozen	2 extra-large eggs
½ cup freshly grated Parmesan cheese (preferably imported)	1 extra-large egg white
	All purpose flour
¼ teaspoon salt	Dry breadcrumbs
¼ teaspoon freshly ground pepper	Vegetable oil (for deep frying)
¼ teaspoon freshly grated nutmeg	The Duke's Tomato Sauce*
¼ teaspoon ground coriander	Freshly grated Parmesan cheese (preferably imported)

Place ricotta in cheesecloth-lined colander. Set over bowl and let drain in refrigerator for 2 hours.

Steam fresh spinach until wilted, about 3 minutes. (Cook frozen spinach in boiling water until just thawed, about 4 minutes.) Drain well. Squeeze excess water out of spinach. Cook peas in medium saucepan of boiling water until just tender, about 6 minutes for fresh or about 1 minute for frozen. Drain well. Return peas to dry pan and stir over medium-high heat until dry, about 1½ minutes. Cool slightly. Puree spinach, peas, ½ cup Parmesan, salt, pepper, nutmeg and coriander in processor until smooth.

Combine ricotta, 2 yolks and 1 egg in large bowl. Mix in 1½ cups breadcrumbs and vegetable puree. Form two 1-inch balls and place on surface touching each other; if vegetable balls stick together, stir more breadcrumbs into mixture 2 tablespoons at a time, testing after each addition. (*Can be prepared 1 day ahead and refrigerated.*)

Beat 2 eggs and 1 white in small bowl to blend. Form spinach mixture into 1¼-inch rounds; flatten to ½ inch thick. Dust with flour. Dip each in egg mixture, then coat with breadcrumbs.

Heat oil in deep fryer to 375°F. Fry rounds in batches until brown and crisp, about 2½ minutes. Drain on paper towels. Transfer to platter and top with tomato sauce. Serve immediately, passing Parmesan separately.

*The Duke's Tomato Sauce

Makes about 4 cups

¼ **pound chicken livers**
3 **28-ounce cans Italian plum tomatoes, drained**

⅓ **cup olive oil**
6 **green onions (white part and ½ inch of green part), thinly sliced**

4 **to 6 small dried red chilies**
1 **¼-pound slice ham, cut into ¼-inch cubes**
¾ **teaspoon salt**
10 **fresh sage leaves, chopped or ½ teaspoon dried, crumbled**

Cover livers with cold water in small saucepan. Bring to boil and cook 10 minutes. Rinse with cold water and drain. Chop finely. Set colander in medium bowl. Halve and seed tomatoes over colander, letting juice collect in bowl. Chop tomatoes.

Heat oil in heavy large skillet over medium-high heat. Add onions and chilies and stir until aromatic, about 2 minutes. Add livers and ham and stir 1 minute. Remove all but 1 chili from skillet, using slotted spoon, and discard. Increase heat to high. When oil sizzles, add tomatoes, juice collected in bowl and salt. Cook until sauce thickens, stirring only when tomatoes stick to pan and reducing heat if necessary to prevent scorching, about 12 minutes. Add sage and cook 2 minutes. (*Can be prepared 1 day ahead. Cool completely, cover and refrigerate. Reheat before using.*)

Gnocchi Roll Florentine Style

*This yellow and green
spiraled roll makes
a festive beginning.*

12 servings

Spinach Filling
5 pounds spinach, stemmed, or four
10-ounce packages frozen
chopped spinach, thawed and
drained

½ cup (1 stick) butter
2 medium garlic cloves (do not
peel), crushed
5 ounces bacon, chopped
Salt and freshly ground pepper

Gnocchi Roll
½ medium onion
2 pounds baking potatoes

1½ cups (or more) all purpose flour
½ cup freshly grated Parmesan
cheese (preferably imported)

Salt and freshly ground pepper
5 egg yolks, beaten to blend

Tomato Sauce with Vodka and
Basil*
¾ cup Sage Butter**
Freshly grated Parmesan cheese
(preferably imported)
Fresh basil leaves

For filling: Rinse fresh spinach thoroughly (do not dry). Gradually add to heavy
large pot over high heat. Cover and cook until just wilted, stirring occasionally,
about 4 minutes. Press gently to remove moisture. Chop. (If using frozen spinach,
do not cook.)

Melt butter in heavy large saucepan over medium heat. Add garlic and cook
until golden brown, stirring occasionally, about 8 minutes. Discard garlic using
slotted spoon. Add bacon to butter and cook until golden brown, stirring occasionally, about 10 minutes. Add spinach and stir 2 minutes. Season with salt and
freshly ground pepper. Cool completely.

For gnocchi: Bring water to boil in base of steamer. Add onion to water.
Place potatoes on steamer rack. Cover and cook until just tender.

Spread 1½ cups flour on work surface. Immediately peel one potato. Press
through ricer onto floured surface. Using 2 large forks, toss potato in flour to
coat well. Repeat with remaining potatoes. Add ½ cup Parmesan, salt and pepper
to potatoes and stir with forks. Gather mixture into mound. Make well in center.
Add yolks to well. Gradually mix into potatoes. Knead gently until tender but
firm dough forms, adding more all purpose flour if sticky, about 1 minute.

Generously flour large kitchen towel. Place dough in center of towel. Lightly
roll to 16 × 20-inch rectangle. Spread filling over dough, leaving ½-inch border.
Using cloth as aid, roll dough up jelly roll fashion, starting at one long end and
making first fold tight. Wrap towel tightly around roll. Twist ends. Tie one end
with twine. Tie second end with twine, then run twine down length of roll, wrap
around end, then run back along other side of roll and secure again. Spiral twine
down length of roll, spacing 1 inch apart. Twist around end, then spiral back
down length, spacing 1 inch apart and angling in opposite direction from first
spiral. Refrigerate roll until well chilled. (*Can be made 1 day ahead.*)

Bring enough salted water to boil in fish poacher or large roasting pan to
cover pasta roll. Add roll to water. Simmer until firm to touch, about 1 hour.
Transfer to heated platter. Cover and let stand 30 minutes.

Preheat broiler. Remove twine and towel from pasta roll. Gently cut into
½- to ¾-inch-thick slices, supporting each with spatula. Spoon tomato sauce
down center of heated broilerproof platter. Arrange slices atop sauce. Drizzle
with Sage Butter. Sprinkle with Parmesan. Broil until heated through, about
3 minutes. Garnish with basil.

*Tomato Sauce with Vodka and Basil

Makes about 10 cups

½ cup (1 stick) butter
⅓ cup olive oil
4 medium garlic cloves, crushed
2 medium onions, finely chopped
2 tablespoons plus 2 teaspoons dried thyme, crumbled
2 bay leaves
½ cup dry white wine

9 pounds tomatoes, cored, coarsely chopped and drained
1 chicken bouillon cube
Salt and freshly ground pepper

¾ cup whipping cream
⅓ cup vodka
15 fresh basil leaves, torn into pieces

Melt butter with oil in heavy large saucepan over medium-low heat. Add garlic and cook until golden brown, stirring occasionally, about 8 minutes. Discard garlic using slotted spoon. Add onions, thyme and bay leaves. Cook until onions are translucent, stirring frequently, about 10 minutes. Add wine and cook until almost evaporated, stirring frequently, about 10 minutes. Add tomatoes and bouillon cube. Simmer until sauce is reduced by ¼, stirring frequently, about 50 minutes. Season with salt and pepper. (*Can be prepared 1 day ahead and refrigerated. Rewarm before continuing.*)

Add cream and vodka and stir until heated through; do not boil. Add basil.

**Sage Butter

Makes about 1½ cups

1½ cups (3 sticks) butter
14 fresh sage leaves, minced or ¾ teaspoon dried, crumbled

Salt

Heat butter with sage in heavy small saucepan over low heat until butter melts and is light golden brown, stirring occasionally. Season with salt.

 *Grains*

Classic Polenta

Use this traditional Italian starter as accompaniment with chicken, veal or lamb.

8 servings

2 quarts chicken stock
½ teaspoon salt or to taste
1 pound Italian polenta or medium grind cornmeal (about 3 cups)

2 tablespoons (¼ stick) butter

Bring stock and salt to boil in heavy 4-quart saucepan. Add polenta in very thin stream, stirring constantly. Reduce heat and simmer until polenta is consistency of thick oatmeal, stirring frequently, about 30 minutes. Mix in butter. Serve immediately.

Sweet Polenta with Ricotta

Sublime as a first course, this delicate polenta can also be served as a side dish with roasts, sausage or poultry.

6 servings

3 cups water
1½ teaspoons salt
1½ cups coarse cornmeal

2 tablespoons (¼ stick) unsalted butter
1 pound ricotta cheese
⅓ cup (1 ounce) grated aged

provolone, caciocavallo or Romano cheese
3 extra-large eggs
2 tablespoons sugar
1 tablespoon butter

Grated aged provolone, caciocavallo or Romano cheese

Bring water and salt to boil in heavy small saucepan. Stir in cornmeal in thin stream. Reduce heat to low, cover partially and cook until polenta is thick enough to hold wooden spoon upright in center of pan, stirring frequently, about 35 minutes.

Stir 2 tablespoons butter into polenta, then ricotta and ⅓ cup provolone. Mix in eggs and sugar. Generously butter 6-cup soufflé dish. Add polenta. Dot with 1 tablespoon butter. (*Can be prepared 2 hours ahead to this point. Let stand at room temperature.*)

Preheat oven to 375°F. Bake polenta until top forms light crust, 35 to 40 minutes. Serve polenta hot, passing grated cheese separately.

Spinach and Polenta Custards with Pimiento Sauce

6 servings

1 cup water
⅓ cup yellow cornmeal

10 ounces fresh spinach, stemmed and rinsed (do not dry)

3 large shallots
2 tablespoons (¼ stick) unsalted butter

¾ cup milk
½ teaspoon salt
Freshly grated nutmeg
Freshly ground pepper
3 eggs

Pimiento Sauce*

Position rack in center of oven and preheat to 350°F. Butter six ⅔-cup soufflé dishes or ramekins.

Bring 1 cup water to boil in heavy 1-quart saucepan. Add cornmeal in thin stream. Cook over medium heat until water is absorbed, stirring constantly, about 5 minutes. Let cool. (*Can be prepared 3 days ahead and refrigerated.*)

Place spinach in heavy large nonaluminum saucepan. Cover and cook over high heat until wilted, about 3 minutes. Drain; rinse under cold water. Wrap in towel and squeeze to remove as much moisture as possible.

With machine running, drop shallots through processor feed tube and mince. Melt butter in heavy 8-inch skillet over low heat. Add shallots and cook until soft, stirring occasionally, about 6 minutes. Set aside.

Process cornmeal mixture in processor until smooth, about 20 seconds. Add shallots, milk, salt, nutmeg and pepper and blend until smooth, about 10 seconds. Add spinach and eggs and blend using 3 to 4 on/off turns. Divide mixture evenly among prepared dishes. Bake until puffed, light golden and tester inserted in centers comes out clean, about 30 minutes. (*Can be prepared 1 day ahead, covered and refrigerated. To reheat, bring to room temperature. Cover custards tightly with foil and bake in 450°F oven 10 to 12 minutes.*)

Spread 1 tablespoon Pimiento Sauce on each plate. Run knife around insides of soufflé dishes. Carefully invert custards atop sauce. Serve hot.

*Pimiento Sauce

Makes about ½ cup

1 4-ounce jar whole pimientos, drained
1 teaspoon raspberry vinegar
⅛ teaspoon salt

⅛ teaspoon sugar
¼ cup (½ stick) well-chilled unsalted butter, cut into 4 pieces

Combine pimientos, vinegar, salt and sugar in processor and puree until smooth. Transfer to small nonaluminum saucepan. Cook over medium heat until warmed through. Whisk in butter 1 piece at a time, incorporating each piece before adding next. Adjust seasoning. (*Can be prepared 20 minutes ahead and kept warm over warm water, or 1 hour ahead and kept warm in vacuum bottle.*)

Golden Carrot Risotto

8 servings

5 to 6 cups chicken stock
5 tablespoons butter
1 medium onion, finely chopped
2½ cups Arborio rice or short-grain pearl rice
1 cup dry white wine
1½ cups finely grated carrots

½ cup freshly grated Parmesan cheese
Pinch of freshly grated nutmeg
Salt and freshly ground white pepper
Freshly grated Parmesan cheese

Bring stock to simmer in small saucepan. Reduce heat to low.

Melt 4 tablespoons butter in heavy medium saucepan over medium heat. Add onion and sauté until pale yellow, about 5 minutes. Add rice and mix to coat with butter. Add wine and stir until wine is evaporated, about 6 minutes. Add enough hot stock to cover, about 3 cups. Reduce heat to low and stir until stock has been absorbed. Continue cooking 10 minutes, stirring and adding ½ cup stock at a time, making sure stock is absorbed before next addition. Add carrots and continue stirring and adding stock until rice is tender but still firm to bite, about 10 minutes. Remove from heat. Stir in remaining 1 tablespoon butter, ½ cup Parmesan, nutmeg, salt and pepper. Serve with additional cheese.

Risotto with Pesto

8 servings

7 cups (about) chicken stock
¼ cup (½ stick) butter
½ cup finely chopped onion
2 cups Arborio rice*
½ cup dry white wine
2 tablespoons (¼ stick) butter, room temperature

5 tablespoons Pesto Sauce**
½ cup freshly grated Parmesan cheese

Bring stock to slow simmer in medium saucepan. Melt ¼ cup butter in another heavy medium saucepan over medium-low heat. Add onion and cook until soft, stirring frequently, about 8 minutes. Add rice and stir until opaque, about 2 minutes. Add wine and simmer until absorbed. Add 2 cups simmering stock and simmer until almost completely absorbed, stirring frequently about 7 minutes. Add 2 more cups simmering stock to rice and cook until almost absorbed, stirring frequently, about 7 minutes. Add remaining stock ½ cup at a time and cook until rice is just tender. Mix in remaining butter and Pesto Sauce. Stir in Parmesan and serve.

*Available at Italian markets.

**Pesto Sauce
_____

Makes about 1²/₃ cups

2 cups packed fresh basil leaves
2 large garlic cloves
³/₄ cup freshly grated Parmesan or
  Romano cheese

¹/₂ cup pine nuts
²/₃ cup olive oil

Blend basil and garlic in processor to fine paste, stopping occasionally to scrape down sides of work bowl. Add cheese and pine nuts and process until well blended. With machine running, pour olive oil through feed tube in slow steady stream and mix until smooth and creamy. Transfer pesto to jar. Cover surface with film of olive oil. Refrigerate up to 3 months or freeze. Stir Pesto Sauce before using.

Risotto with Shrimp, Mussels and Peas
_____

6 servings

1¹/₂ pounds mussels, scrubbed and
  debearded

1 cup uncooked shrimp, shelled and
  deveined

4 tablespoons (¹/₂ stick) butter
1 medium onion, chopped
1 garlic clove, minced

3 cups (about) fish stock
1¹/₂ cups Arborio rice*
¹/₂ cup fresh or frozen, thawed peas
3 tablespoons minced fresh parsley
1 tablespoon grated lemon peel
  Salt and freshly ground pepper

Fill large pot with ¹/₂ inch water. Add mussels. Cover and steam over medium-high heat 5 minutes. Remove and discard unopened mussels. Cook remaining mussels about 5 more minutes. Ladle liquid through strainer lined with several layers of dampened cheesecloth. Reserve liquid. Remove mussels from shells. Rinse and reserve shells.

Gently simmer shrimp in enough water to cover in small saucepan until just opaque, about 2 minutes. Drain, reserving cooking liquid.

Melt 3 tablespoons butter in heavy medium saucepan over medium-low heat. Add onion and garlic and cook until translucent, stirring mixture occasionally, about 10 minutes.

Combine reserved mussel and shrimp liquid in measuring cup. Add enough fish stock to total 5 cups. Transfer to another saucepan and bring to simmer. Add rice to onion mixture and stir until opaque, about 2 minutes. Increase heat to medium. Add ¹/₂ cup simmering liquid, and cook until almost completely absorbed, stirring constantly. Continue adding simmering liquid, ¹/₂ cup at a time and stirring constantly, until rice is tender yet firm to bite, about 30 minutes (risotto should be creamy but not mushy). Stir in mussels, shrimp, remaining 1 tablespoon butter and peas and heat through. Remove from heat. Stir in parsley and lemon peel. Season with salt and pepper. Mound on platter. Garnish with mussel shells.

*Available at Italian markets.

Meatball and Rice Timbale

6 servings

Meatballs
- 1 cup fresh breadcrumbs
- ½ pound ground beef
- ¼ cup minced fresh parsley
- 3 tablespoons freshly grated Parmesan cheese
- 1 egg, beaten to blend
  - Salt and freshly ground pepper
  - Freshly grated nutmeg
  - All purpose flour
- ⅓ cup olive oil

Filling
- 1 ounce dried porcini mushrooms

- ½ pound sweet Italian sausage
- ¼ cup water

- 2 tablespoons (¼ stick) butter
- 2 tablespoons chopped onion
- ½ cup frozen peas
- ½ pound chicken livers, trimmed and cut into ½-inch pieces
- ½ cup Quick Tomato Sauce*

Rice
- 5 quarts water
- 2 teaspoons salt
- 12 ounces Arborio rice**
- 1 cup Quick Tomato Sauce
- 1 cup freshly grated Parmesan cheese
- ¼ cup (½ stick) butter
- 2 eggs, beaten to blend
  - Salt and freshly ground pepper

Assembly
- 1 cup (about) dry breadcrumbs
- 6 ounces mozzarella cheese, diced
- 2 hard-cooked eggs, thinly sliced
- 2 tablespoons (¼ stick) butter
  - Quick Tomato Sauce

For meatballs: Mix breadcrumbs, beef, parsley, Parmesan, egg, salt, pepper and nutmeg. Roll by rounded teaspoonfuls into meatballs. Dredge lightly in flour, shaking off excess. Heat oil in heavy large skillet over medium-high heat. Add meatballs in batches (do not crowd) and brown well on all sides, about 5 minutes. Remove using slotted spoon and drain thoroughly on paper towels.

For filling: Soak mushrooms in warm water to cover until softened, about 30 minutes. Drain, reserving soaking liquid. Pat mushrooms dry; chop finely, discarding any hard parts.

Pierce sausage all over. Combine sausage with water in skillet and simmer gently until water evaporates and sausage is cooked through, turning sausage frequently, about 15 minutes. Cut sausage into ½-inch pieces.

Melt butter in same skillet over medium-low heat. Add mushrooms and onion and cook until onion is tender, stirring occasionally, about 5 minutes. Add reserved mushroom liquid and peas and cook until liquid has evaporated and peas are tender, stirring occasionally, about 5 minutes. Add livers and stir 2 minutes. Add meatballs, sausage and tomato sauce and cook 2 minutes to blend flavors.

For rice: Bring water with salt to boil. Stir in rice and cook until tender but still firm to bite, about 15 minutes. Drain. Toss immediately with tomato sauce, Parmesan, butter and eggs. Season with salt and pepper. Cool.

To assemble: Preheat oven to 375°F. Butter 3-quart soufflé dish or timbale mold. Coat dish completely with breadcrumbs; reserve remaining crumbs. Press ⅔ of rice mixture onto bottom and up sides of mold. Top with half of mozzarella. Cover with half of filling. Arrange eggs over. Top with remaining mozzarella. Cover with remaining filling. Spread remaining rice mixture over, pressing gently. Sprinkle with enough of remaining breadcrumbs to cover completely. Dot with butter. (*Can be prepared 1 day ahead and refrigerated. Bring to room temperature before baking.*) Bake until top is brown and crusty, about 40 minutes. Let cool 10 minutes. Unmold onto platter. Cut into wedges. Pass remaining tomato sauce separately.

*Quick Tomato Sauce

Makes 2²/₃ cups

2 tablespoons (¹/₄ stick) butter	2 28-ounce cans Italian plum
4 ounces prosciutto fat or ham fat, chopped	tomatoes, drained and chopped
	Salt and freshly ground pepper
1 small onion, chopped	Pinch of sugar

Melt butter in heavy large saucepan over medium-low heat. Add fat and onion and cook until fat is rendered and onion is soft, stirring occasionally, about 8 minutes. Add tomatoes, salt, pepper and sugar and boil until reduced 2²/₃ cups, 45 minutes. (*Can be prepared 2 days ahead and refrigerated.*)

**Available at Italian markets.

Rice with Artichokes and Olives

4 to 6 servings

Artichokes
  2 artichokes
  1 lemon, halved
  4 cups water
    Juice of 1 lemon

Rice
¹/₄ cup (¹/₂ stick) butter
  1 medium onion, thinly sliced
1¹/₂ cups Arborio rice or long-grain
    rice

  2 cups chicken stock, heated
  2 cups beef stock, heated

  3 tablespoons olive oil
12 green Sicilian olives, pitted and
    thinly sliced
    Salt and freshly ground pepper

For artichokes: Wash and drain artichokes. Remove any tough outer leaves. Cut off stems and trim. Slice stems into thin rounds. Rub lemon over each slice to prevent discoloring. Combine water and lemon juice in large bowl. Add stem rounds. Cut artichokes lengthwise and with melon scoop or sturdy teaspoon, remove and discard fuzzy choke, scraping to clean thoroughly. Cut artichokes into thin wedges and rub with lemon. As each artichoke is cleaned, drop into acidulated water. Set aside.

    For rice: Melt butter in large saucepan over medium-high heat. Add onion and sauté until translucent. Stir in rice and cook until grains crackle. Add hot broths, stirring once. Reduce heat to medium-low, cover and cook, stirring twice, approximately 10 minutes.

    Heat olive oil and olives in medium saucepan over medium-high heat. Drain artichoke wedges and stems thoroughly and pat dry. Add to skillet and sauté until crisp-tender, about 6 minutes. Stir artichoke mixture into rice. Cook, uncovered, until rice is tender and liquid is evaporated. Season with salt and pepper and serve immediately.

 *Breads*

Maria's Focaccia

8 servings

1 10-ounce boiling potato, peeled

1 tablespoon dry yeast
½ cup warm water (105°F to 115°F)

3 tablespoons bread flour

2 tablespoons minced fresh
   rosemary
2 tablespoons minced garlic
2 tablespoons olive oil

7 cups (about) bread flour
1 tablespoon salt

Olive oil

2 tablespoons olive oil
Coarse kosher salt
Freshly ground pepper

Cover potato with cold water in medium saucepan. Simmer until potato is tender. Drain, reserving cooking liquid. Mash potato or press through ricer. Measure 1 cup potato.

Meanwhile, sprinkle yeast over ½ cup warm water in small bowl; stir to dissolve. Let stand 5 minutes. Mix in 3 tablespoons flour. Cover bowl with plastic wrap and let stand in warm draft-free area for 30 minutes.

Blanch rosemary and garlic in small saucepan of boiling water 1 minute. Strain. Add enough water to potato liquid to measure 2 cups. Mix in rosemary, garlic and 2 tablespoons oil.

Combine 6½ cups flour and 1 tablespoon salt in large bowl. Stir down yeast mixture and add to flour with herb-water mixture and 1 cup potato. Mix until sticky dough forms. Knead on well-floured surface until dough is smooth and elastic, adding more flour if sticky, about 10 minutes.

Oil large bowl. Add dough, turning to coat entire surface. Cover bowl with plastic. Let dough rise in warm draft-free area until doubled, 1½ hours.

Punch dough down. Knead on lightly floured surface until smooth, about 2 minutes. Cover; let rest 10 minutes.

Grease rimmed 9 × 13-inch jelly roll pan. Roll dough out on lightly floured surface to 9 × 13-inch rectangle. Transfer to prepared pan. Brush top with 2 tablespoons oil. Sprinkle lightly with coarse salt and generously with pepper. Let rise in warm draft-free area until almost doubled, 1¼ hours.

Preheat oven to 400°F. Bake until bread is brown and sounds hollow when tapped, about 40 minutes. Cool in pan 10 minutes. Transfer bread to rack and let cool completely.

Italian Country Bread

*Makes 2 loaves, or 1 loaf
and about 15 deep-
fried rolls (see page 114)*

Cornmeal
2½ cups warm water (105°F to 115°F)
4 envelopes dry yeast
1 tablespoon sugar

4 to 5 cups unbleached all purpose
   flour
2 to 3 cups whole wheat flour
1 tablespoon salt

Set baking stones* in oven and sprinkle with cornmeal. Oil large bowl and set aside. Combine warm water, yeast and sugar in another large bowl. Let stand until foamy, about 5 minutes. Blend in 4 cups all purpose flour and 2 cups whole wheat flour with salt. Add more of each flour to make workable dough. Turn out onto lightly floured surface and knead until smooth, about 10 minutes. Form dough into ball. Dust with flour. Transfer to prepared bowl, turning to coat entire surface. Cover with towel and let stand in warm draft-free area until doubled in volume, about 40 to 45 minutes.

Punch dough down. Turn out onto work surface and divide in half. Shape each half into round or oblong loaf. Transfer to prepared baking stones. Cut 3 or 4 diagonal slashes into top of each loaf using sharp knife or razor blade. Brush loaves with water. Set oven temperature to 350°F and bake until loaves are golden and sound hollow when tapped, about 1 hour. Transfer loaves to racks to cool completely before slicing and storing.

*If unavailable, bread can also be prepared on large baking sheets sprinkled with cornmeal. Do not preheat oven.

Pepper Bread

This easy-to-make bread has tiny bits of crisp salt pork and the zesty bite of cracked black pepper.

Makes 2 loaves

1 **pound salt pork, diced**

2¼ **cups warm water (105°F to 115°F)**

1 **tablespoon salt**

2 **teaspoons coarsely cracked black pepper**

2 **envelopes dry yeast**

6½ **to 7 cups unbleached all purpose flour**

1 **egg, lightly beaten**
   Coarse salt (optional)

Oil large bowl and set aside. Warm salt pork in heavy large skillet over low heat until some fat is rendered. Increase heat to medium-high and sauté until crisp. Drain pork on paper towels. Reserve ¼ cup fat from skillet.

Combine 1½ cups warm water, reserved pork fat, salt and pepper in large bowl. Dissolve yeast in remaining ¾ cup warm water. Let stand until foamy and proofed, about 10 minutes. Add to pepper mixture. Add salt pork and 3 cups flour, stirring vigorously until mixture forms smooth batter. Blend in remaining flour 1 cup at a time to form stiff dough. Turn out onto lightly floured surface and knead until smooth and elastic, about 10 minutes. Transfer to prepared bowl, turning to coat entire surface. Cover and let stand in warm draft-free area until doubled in volume, about 1 hour.

Punch dough down. Turn out onto lightly floured surface and cut in half. Divide each half into thirds. Roll each piece into 12-inch-long rope. Place 3 ropes on ungreased baking sheet and braid together, pinching ends to seal. Repeat with remaining dough. Cover lightly and let stand in warm, draft-free area until doubled, about 45 minutes.

Preheat oven to 375°F. Brush loaves with beaten egg. Sprinkle with coarse salt. Bake until crust is golden brown and bread sounds hollow when tapped, 40 to 45 minutes. Cool on racks. (*Italian Pepper Bread can be prepared ahead, wrapped tightly in foil and frozen.*)

Basil and Sage Bread

Makes 2 baguettes

1 envelope dry yeast
1 cup warm water (105°F to 115°F)
5½ cups (or more) all purpose flour

¼ cup olive oil
4 teaspoons dried basil, crumbled
¼ teaspoon dried sage, crumbled
½ cup dry white wine

1¾ teaspoons salt
¼ teaspoon freshly ground pepper
½ cup warm water (105°F to 115°F)

Sprinkle yeast over 1 cup water in bowl of heavy-duty electric mixer; stir to dissolve. Let stand 5 minutes. Thoroughly mix in 1½ cups flour. Sprinkle ½ cup flour over dough. Cover with towel. Let rise in warm draft-free area until doubled, about 1½ hours.

Heat oil in heavy small skillet over low heat. Add basil and sage and stir until aromatic, about 1 minute. Cool. Blend 1 cup flour, oil mixture, wine, salt and pepper into dough, using dough hook. Slowly add remaining ½ cup water. Stir in 2½ cups flour ½ cup at a time. Knead dough in mixer until smooth and resilient, about 10 minutes, adding more all purpose flour if sticky. Grease large bowl. Add dough, turning to coat entire surface. Cover bowl. Let dough rise in warm draft-free area until doubled, about 1¼ hours.

Grease two baking sheets. Punch dough down. Divide in half. Form each piece into 14-inch-long loaf. Place on prepared sheets, seam side down. Let rise in warm draft-free area until almost doubled, about 1 hour.

Preheat oven to 400°F. Slash tops of loaves with sharp knife. Bake until breads sound hollow when tapped on bottom, about 50 minutes. Cool on wire racks before serving.

Ricotta Cheese Bread

This versatile loaf can be made sweet with the addition of candied fruit or savory with chopped fresh herbs. It is excellent plain or toasted.

Makes one 9 × 5-inch loaf or two 7 × 3 × 2-inch loaves

¼ cup milk, scalded and cooled to 105°F to 115°F
1 tablespoon dry yeast
1 tablespoon sugar for savory loaf or ¼ cup sugar for sweet loaf
6 tablespoons (¾ stick) butter, softened
2 eggs, room temperature
2 teaspoons salt
1½ cups ricotta cheese
¼ cup mixed chopped fresh herbs (parsley, chives, marjoram, basil, rosemary, oregano)

or
1 cup mixed candied fruit and ¼ cup raisins soaked in 2 tablespoons rum
1 teaspoon vanilla
Generous pinch of freshly grated nutmeg

3 to 4 cups all purpose flour

1 egg yolk blended with 2 tablespoons milk

Stir milk, yeast and sugar in large bowl until yeast dissolves. Let stand 20 minutes. Beat in butter, eggs and salt until smooth. Blend in ricotta and herbs for savory loaf, or ricotta and candied fruit, raisins, vanilla and nutmeg for sweet loaf. Beat in 3 cups flour until smooth and slightly elastic, about 5 minutes. If mixture appears too moist, beat in up to 1 cup more flour. Dough should be soft but not dry. Transfer to buttered bowl, turning to coat entire surface. Cover dough and let rise in warm draft-free area until doubled, about 1½ hours.

Punch dough down. Let rise again in warm draft-free area until doubled.

Butter 9 × 5-inch loaf pan. Punch dough down. Form into smooth loaf and place in prepared pan. Let rise ⅔ up pan. Brush loaf with egg glaze.

Preheat oven to 375°F. Bake loaf 50 minutes. Let cool in pan 5 minutes, then invert loaf onto rack.

For 2 small loaves: Divide dough in half and bake in two 7 × 3 × 2-inch pans. You can also create 2 small loaves of each type at once. Make dough with savory sponge. After adding ricotta, divide dough in half. Add 2 tablespoons chopped fresh herbs to 1 portion. To other portion, add ½ cup candied fruit, 2 tablespoons sugar, 2 tablespoons raisins, ½ teaspoon vanilla and pinch of freshly grated nutmeg.

Grilled Garlic Bread

10 to 12 appetizer servings

1 large round loaf Italian Country Bread (see page 45) or French bread

2 to 3 large garlic cloves, halved
Green virgin olive oil

Prepare charcoal grill or preheat broiler. Cut bread into thick slices. Arrange on grill or broiler rack and toast on both sides. Immediately rub with cut garlic clove. Transfer to platter. Drizzle liberally with oil and serve.

4 ❦ Fish and Shellfish

It should come as no surprise that Italy, a peninsula surrounded by seas, striped with rivers and dotted with lakes, is a country devoted to the preparation and consumption of fish and shellfish. From the waters of the Mediterranean, Adriatic, Tyrrhenian, Ionian and Ligurian seas; the Po and Arno rivers; and lakes Garda, Maggiore, Lugano and Como come such sea creatures as anchovies, mullet, sea bream, John Dory, eel, mackerel, sardines, tuna, bass, snapper, swordfish, scallops, scampi, gamberi, squid, cuttlefish, octopus, sea urchins, numerous kinds of mussels and clams, sole, salmon, shad, perch, trout, pike, sturgeon—plus many, many more. Bustling fish markets are the highlight of many coastal cities, especially Venice and Genoa.

Some of the delectable seafood dishes included in our collection of recipes are Grilled Shrimp with Anchovy Caper Sauce (page 55), Salmon Wrapped in Radicchio (page 50), Steamed Clams and Mussels with Italian Sausage (page 55) and Italian-style Shrimp with Pernod (page 56).

Although Italy is blessed with an amazing bounty of fresh fish, it is nonetheless enamored of a preserved fish called baccalà (salt cod). You can try it by using the recipes for Crisp-fried Salt Cod (page 53) and Tricolored Baccalà (page 52).

Salmon Wrapped in Radicchio

4 servings

³/₄ cup dry white wine
³/₄ cup white wine vinegar
8 large shallots, minced

2 tablespoons dry white wine
1 1¹/₂-pound fillet of salmon tail, skinned and cut into 4 pieces
Salt and freshly ground pepper
8 large radicchio leaves (tough ribs removed), blanched and patted dry
2 tablespoons (¹/₄ stick) butter
1 tablespoon snipped fresh chives

2 tablespoons (¹/₄ stick) butter, melted
3 tablespoons whipping cream
3 tablespoons fresh lemon juice
1 tablespoon water
1¹/₂ cups (3 sticks) unsalted butter
2 tablespoons chopped watercress leaves

Boil ³/₄ cup wine and vinegar with shallots in heavy medium saucepan until liquid vaporates. Reserve 5 tablespoons shallots.

Preheat oven to 375°F. Butter baking sheet. Sprinkle sheet with 2 tablespoons wine. Season salmon on both sides with salt and pepper. Overlap 2 radicchio leaves. Top with 1 piece of salmon. Dot with ¹/₂ tablespoon butter. Sprinkle with some of chives. Fold in short ends of radicchio. Roll salmon in radicchio to enclose completely. Repeat with remaining salmon. Arrange seam side down on prepared sheet. Brush with melted butter. Cover with parchment. Bake until cooked through, about 10 minutes.

Meanwhile, combine reserved shallots, cream, lemon juice, water and salt in same saucepan and bring to boil. Reduce heat to low. Whisk in butter 1 tablespoon at a time. Stir in watercress. Season with salt and pepper. Arrange 1 salmon roll on each plate. Spoon sauce over. Serve immediately.

Monkfish with Leeks and Olives

4 servings

4 tablespoons olive oil
2 medium leeks, white and light green parts only, halved lengthwise and cut into 3 × ¹/₈-inch strips

1¹/₂ pounds monkfish fillet (about 3 inches thick), skinned, trimmed and cut crosswise into 2 to 3 pieces
3 tablespoons all purpose flour
2 tablespoons (¹/₄ stick) unsalted butter
1 medium celery stalk, diced
1 small carrot, diced
1 small onion, chopped

4 medium garlic cloves, chopped
1¹/₂ pounds tomatoes, unpeeled, cut into eighths
²/₃ cup Simple Fish Stock*
1 bay leaf
1 large thyme sprig or ¹/₄ teaspoon dried, crumbled
Salt and freshly ground pepper

1 teaspoon tomato paste
³/₄ cup pitted black olives, drained
¹/₂ cup pitted green olives, drained

Heat 2 tablespoons oil in heavy large skillet over low heat. Add leeks, cover and cook until tender, stirring occasionally, about 10 minutes.

Pat fish dry. Dredge in flour, shaking off excess. Melt butter with remaining oil in heavy large skillet over medium-high heat. Add fish and brown lightly on all sides. Transfer to plate. Reduce heat to low. Stir in celery, carrot, onion and garlic, scraping up browned bits, and cook until softened, about 3 minutes. Return fish to skillet. Add tomatoes, stock, bay leaf, thyme, salt and pepper and bring to boil. Reduce heat to low, cover and cook 7 minutes. Turn fish over and cook until skewer pierces fish easily and comes out hot, about 8 minutes. Transfer fish to platter. Cover and keep warm.

Using spoon, crush tomatoes in skillet. Simmer until very soft, stirring frequently, about 10 minutes. Strain sauce, pressing firmly on solids to extract as much liquid as possible. Return sauce to skillet and boil until reduced to 1½ cups. Blend in tomato paste. Stir in leeks and olives and cook 1 minute. Adjust seasoning.

To serve, cut fish into ½- to ¾-inch-thick slices. Return to sauce. Cover and warm through. Arrange fish on platter or plates. Spoon sauce over.

*Simple Fish Stock

Makes about 1 quart

1½ **pounds bones, tails and heads from nonoily fish or 1 pound fish pieces for chowder**

1 **tablespoon unsalted butter**
1 **medium onion, sliced**

5 **parsley stems**
1 **bay leaf**
1 **thyme sprig or pinch of dried, crumbled**

Rinse fish bones under cold running water at least 5 minutes.

Melt butter in large saucepan over low heat. Add onion and cook until softened, stirring occasionally, about 5 minutes. Add bones, remaining ingredients and water to cover. Bring to boil, skimming foam from surface. Reduce heat and simmer for 20 minutes, skimming occasionally. Strain through fine sieve without pressing on solids. Refrigerate until ready to use (*Can be prepared 1 day ahead.*)

Fillet of Sole Saltato

4 servings

1 **pound sole fillets (or any firm-fleshed white fish fillets), cut into 1½-inch squares**
½ **teaspoon salt**
¼ **teaspoon freshly ground white pepper**
2 **tablespoons all purpose flour**

Juice of 1 lemon
1 **tablespoon sugar**
1 **tablespoon dry white wine or vermouth**

2 **tablespoons vegetable oil**
1 **celery stalk, minced**

Sprinkle fish with salt and pepper. Dust with flour, shaking off excess.

Combine lemon juice, sugar and wine in small saucepan over low heat and cook until sugar is dissolved and sauce is reduced by half. Remove sauce from heat and set aside; keep warm.

Place large skillet over high heat until very hot, about 30 seconds. Add oil, coating bottom evenly. Add celery and stir-fry about 2 minutes. Add fish and continue stirring until it is firm and white, about 3 minutes. Turn onto heated platter. Pour lemon sauce over and serve immediately.

Sole a la Despina

2 to 4 servings

5 tablespoons butter
1 tablespoon olive oil
4 sole fillets (about 1 pound)
  All purpose flour
2 eggs, beaten to blend
1/4 cup slivered almonds, toasted

1/4 cup dry white wine
2 tablespoons fresh lemon juice
  Lemon wedges

Melt 4 tablespoons butter with oil in large skillet over medium-high heat. Dip fillets in flour, then in beaten eggs. Add to skillet and cook until browned and just cooked through, 2 to 3 minutes per side. Transfer to serving platter; keep warm.

Melt remaining 1 tablespoon butter in same skillet, scraping up browned bits. Add almonds and cook until heated through, about 1 minute. Add wine and lemon juice and simmer until slightly thickened, stirring constantly. Pour over fish. Garnish with lemon wedges and serve.

Whole Fish with Vegetables

Couscous or potatoes baked in olive oil would be a good accompaniment.

10 servings

Olive oil
1 6-to 7-pound whole salmon, red snapper or bluefish
2 teaspoons salt
2 teaspoons freshly ground pepper
1 teaspoon ground coriander

4 large carrots, peeled
2 mint sprigs
1 large celery heart, cut into 1/4 × 2 1/2-inch strips
2 large tomatoes, cut into 1/4-inch-thick slices

1 large onion, cut into 1/4-inch-thick slices
10 large black Greek olives, rinsed and pitted
10 large green Greek olives, rinsed and pitted
1/3 cup minced fresh parsley
3 garlic cloves, slivered
1/4 cup olive oil

Preheat oven to 375°F. Generously coat large baking pan with olive oil. Place fish in pan and coat inside and out generously with oil. Season inside and out with 1 teaspoon salt, 1 teaspoon pepper and coriander.

Cut carrots crosswise into 3 pieces, then cut lengthwise into 1/4-inch-thick slices. Place mint in fish cavity, then add half of carrots, celery, tomatoes, onion, olives, parsley and garlic. Cover fish with remaining carrots, celery, onion, olives, parsley and garlic. Line up remaining tomatoes on top. Sprinkle with remaining 1 teaspoon salt and pepper. Drizzle with 1/4 cup oil. Bake until fish is just opaque, about 10 minutes per pound.

Crisp-fried Salt Cod

4 servings

1 pound baccalà (salt cod),*
   cut into 3 × 5-inch pieces

¼ cup olive oil
2 tablespoons vegetable oil
3 garlic cloves, crushed
¼ cup diced (⅛-inch) prosciutto fat
   with rind or salt pork

All purpose flour
¼ teaspoon freshly ground pepper
3 tablespoons fresh lemon juice
   Lemon wedges

Soak salt cod in water to cover in cool place for 24 hours, changing water at least 6 times to remove salt.

Drain fish; rinse well and pat dry. Heat both oils in heavy large skillet over medium-low heat. Add garlic and prosciutto fat and cook until garlic is lightly browned and fat rendered, about 10 minutes. Discard garlic and any unmelted fat, using slotted spoon. Increase heat to medium-high. Combine flour and pepper on plate. Dip fish in flour to coat lightly. Add fish to skillet and cook until golden and just beginning to flake, turning once, about 9 minutes per 1-inch thickness. Transfer to heated platter. Discard all but ¼ cup drippings in pan. Stir lemon juice into skillet. Pour over fish. Garnish with lemon and serve.

*Available at Italian markets.

Tricolored Baccalà

Baccalà is cod that has been dried in the sun and preserved in salt.

8 servings

2 pounds baccalà (salt cod)*

1 medium onion, quartered
1 celery stalk, halved
1 bunch parsley

2 to 3 anchovies
1 sour pickle or 3 to 4 cornichons
1 large shallot
1 large garlic clove
1 tablespoon capers, rinsed and
   drained

1 tablespoon white wine vinegar
½ cup olive oil
1 small boiling potato, peeled,
   cooked and quartered
1 2-ounce jar pimiento strips,
   drained

Soak baccalà in water to cover 48 hours, changing water every 8 hours. Drain fish thoroughly.

Combine fish, onion, celery, 3 parsley sprigs and water to cover in stockpot and bring to boil. Reduce heat and simmer 10 minutes. Cool to room temperature in liquid. Drain; discard vegetables. Skin and bone fish. Cut along grain into 2-inch pieces. Arrange on serving platter.

Finely chop 2 parsley sprigs, anchovies, pickle, shallot, garlic and capers with vinegar in processor using several on/off turns. With machine running, slowly pour oil through feed tube, adding potato as sauce thickens. Spoon sauce over fish. Garnish with pimiento and parsley. Serve at room temperature.

*Available at Italian markets.

Calamari fra Diavolo

A delicious "deviled" squid.

2 to 3 servings

1 cup minced carrot
⅓ cup minced celery
2 teaspoons minced garlic
2 tablespoons olive oil
1½ cups peeled, seeded and chopped
   tomato
½ cup chopped fresh basil
3 tablespoons tomato paste
1 teaspoon dried oregano,
   crumbled

¼ teaspoon freshly ground pepper
¼ teaspoon dried red pepper flakes
   Salt

2 pounds squid, cleaned and sliced
   into ¾-inch rings
   Freshly cooked pasta

Sauté carrot, celery and garlic in olive oil in medium skillet over low heat until tender, about 20 minutes. Increase heat to medium-low. Add chopped tomato, fresh basil, tomato paste and seasonings and simmer until sauce is very thick, about 20 minutes.

Reduce heat to low. Add squid and simmer until cooked through, stirring frequently, 10 to 12 minutes. Spoon over pasta and serve immediately.

Crab- and Spinach-stuffed Squid

2 servings

8 small squid (about 1 pound)

1 tablespoon butter
1 tablespoon olive oil
1 garlic clove, minced
2½ ounces stemmed and cleaned
   spinach, chopped (3 cups)
4 ounces crabmeat
   Salt and freshly ground pepper

½ cup dry white wine

All purpose flour

Oil (for deep frying)

Herb Pasta with Double Tomato
Sauce (see page 23)

To clean squid, separate head and tentacles by pulling away from body. Pull out and discard clear, diamond-shaped skeleton. Peel away skin and discard. Cut off tentacles attached to head and reserve; discard head. Rinse out body cavity. Repeat with remaining squid.

Melt butter with oil in medium skillet over medium-low heat. Add garlic and cook until it releases fragrance and just begins to turn golden, about 2 minutes. Add spinach and toss just until wilted. Stir in crabmeat. Season with salt and pepper. Let cool slightly.

Preheat oven to 350°F. Fill squid cavities with crab. Arrange in baking dish. Pour wine over. Bake 20 minutes, basting occasionally with wine.

Meanwhile, coat reserved squid tentacles lightly with flour, shaking off excess. Heat oil in medium saucepan to 375°F. Add tentacles and fry until crisp and golden brown, about 1 to 2 minutes. Drain on paper towels.

Arrange stuffed squid in spoke pattern around Herb Pasta with Double Tomato Sauce. Top pasta with deep-fried tentacles. Serve immediately.

Steamed Clams and Mussels with Italian Sausage

2 servings; can be doubled or tripled

1 large tomato, seeded and chopped
4 teaspoons thinly sliced fresh basil
1 tablespoon thinly sliced fresh oregano
1 teaspoon olive oil
3/4 pound hot Italian sausages
1 large leek (white part only), halved and thinly sliced
1/4 teaspoon dried red pepper flakes
1 8-ounce bottle clam juice
1/2 cup dry white wine

1 tablespoon tomato paste
1 tablespoon Pernod
1 strip orange peel
Freshly ground pepper
1 1/2 pounds clams, scrubbed
3/4 pound mussels, scrubbed and debearded

Combine tomato, basil and oregano in small bowl. Heat oil in heavy large saucepan over medium heat. Add sausages and sauté until brown and cooked through, about 10 minutes. Transfer to paper towels, using tongs or slotted spoon. Pour off all but 1 1/2 tablespoons fat from pan. Add leek to pan and cook until tender, stirring frequently, about 10 minutes. Add pepper flakes and stir 30 seconds. Blend in clam juice, wine, tomato paste, Pernod and orange peel. Increase heat and bring to boil. Season with freshly ground pepper. Place clams in mixture. Cover and steam 3 minutes. Add mussels to saucepan. Cover and steam until shells open, shaking saucepan occasionally, about 5 minutes.

Cut sausages into 1/2-inch-thick pieces. Transfer shellfish to large bowl. Top with sausages and tomatoes.

Grilled Shrimp with Anchovy Caper Sauce

6 servings

9 teaspoons capers, drained
6 large garlic cloves
1/2 teaspoon salt
1/2 cup fresh lemon juice
4 teaspoons olive oil

24 large uncooked shrimp

1 cup plus 1 tablespoon well-chilled unsalted butter
5 anchovies, coarsely chopped
2/3 cup dry white wine
1 tablespoon whipping cream

On cutting board, mince together 8 teaspoons capers, 4 garlic cloves and salt until mixture is almost puree. Transfer to small nonaluminum bowl. Stir in 1/4 cup lemon juice and oil.

To butterfly shrimp, slice 3/4 way through rounded side to 1/4 inch from tail; do not cut through shell. Open shrimp, flattening gently. Spread undersides of shrimp with caper mixture. Let stand 30 minutes.

Mince remaining 2 garlic cloves. Melt 1 tablespoon butter in heavy medium saucepan over medium heat. Add garlic and stir 2 minutes. Add anchovies and stir 1 minute. Add remaining 1/4 cup lemon juice and white wine and boil until reduced to 1 tablespoon. Whisk in cream. Remove from heat. Whisk in 2 tablespoons butter. Set pan over low heat and whisk in remaining butter 1 tablespoon at a time, removing pan from heat briefly if drops of melted butter appear. (*Can be prepared several hours ahead and held in vacuum bottle.*) Stir in remaining capers.

Meanwhile, prepare grill (high heat). Grill shrimp until opaque, about 2 minutes on each side.

To serve, spoon sauce onto plates. Top each with grilled shrimp.

Italian-style Shrimp with Pernod

6 to 8 servings

3 cups canned Italian plum tomatoes, drained and chopped
1/3 cup water
2 tablespoons tomato paste
1/2 teaspoon chopped fresh basil or 1/4 teaspoon dried, crumbled
1/2 teaspoon chopped fresh oregano or 1/4 teaspoon dried, crumbled
1/2 cup olive oil
3 large garlic cloves, minced
1 tablespoon minced fresh ginger
1/4 cup clam juice
1 1/2 tablespoons capers, drained and chopped
1/2 teaspoon dried red pepper flakes

3 tablespoons butter
1 1/2 cups sliced mushrooms
1 cup chopped green bell pepper
1/2 cup chopped onion
1 1/2 pounds large shrimp, shelled and deveined
1/4 cup freshly grated Parmesan cheese
2 tablespoons Pernod

Simmer tomatoes, water and tomato paste in heavy large saucepan over medium-low heat, stirring occasionally, 1 hour. Add basil and oregano and continue simmering 15 minutes. Heat olive oil in another large saucepan over medium-high heat. Add garlic and ginger and sauté 30 seconds. Blend in tomato mixture, clam juice, capers and red pepper flakes. Cover and bring to boil. Remove from heat and set aside.

Preheat oven to 350°F. Melt 1 1/2 tablespoons butter in large skillet over medium-high heat. Sauté mushrooms, bell pepper and onion until most of liquid has evaporated, about 15 minutes. Stir in tomato mixture. Melt remaining butter in another large skillet over high heat. Add shrimp and sauté until just pink, about 1 minute. Remove shrimp and drain on paper towels. Spoon 1 cup tomato sauce into 8 × 12-inch baking dish, spreading evenly. Top with layer of shrimp. Repeat twice with remaining sauce and shrimp. Sprinkle Parmesan over top. Bake until shrimp are tender and cheese is golden brown, about 20 minutes. Warm Pernod in small saucepan. Ignite and pour over shrimp. Serve immediately.

Irwin Horowitz

Left to right: Whole Wheat Fettuccine with Country Ham and Watercress; Veal Shanks Braised in Red Wine and Garlic with Deep-Fried Zucchini and Eggplant; Lemon-Raisin Tart

Irwin Horowitz

From left to right: Red Pepper Soup with Bruschetta; Zucchini and Calamari Salad; Grilled Chicken Paillards with Sage and Fontina Cheese; Peach and Frangelico Gratin

Irwin Horowitz

Italian Almond Cake

Cabbage Soup with Fontina;
Ricotta Cheese Bread

Paul Elson

Irwin Horowitz

Clockwise from bottom right: In the white plate, Neapolitan Steaks, Baked Onions with Red Wine Vinegar and Slow-Simmered Tomatoes with Herbs; Three-Cheese Ravioli with Sage Butter Sauce; Plum and Almond Tart

From top left: Sweet Semolina Diamonds; Zucchini Tube Cake; Mary Tassiello's Ricotta Cake

Irwin Horowitz

5 🍎 Poultry and Game

Italian chicken dishes have always had worldwide appeal. Easy to prepare and immensely flavorful, their variety and number are probably greater than for any other meat. The leghorn breed of chicken from Livorno in Tuscany is the preferred type throughout Italy. Mostly white in color with signature yellow legs, it has been exported and is now bred all over the world. Since it is regarded in Italy as *the* best chicken, when people say "he (or she) has yellow legs," they are referring to a quality person. Some of our quality chicken recipes include Grilled Chicken Paillards with Sage and Fontina Cheese (page 58), Spicy Chicken with Olives and Anchovies (page 59), Hunter's Chicken (page 59) and Stuffed Boneless Chicken with Tarragon Sauce (page 61).

One of the most popular forms of poultry in Italy today is turkey. First brought to Europe from America by the Spaniards in 1519, it reached Italy shortly thereafter. Many old Italian recipes calling for peacock meat were adapted to this relative newcomer. For your dining pleasure, we offer a recipe for Rolled Turkey Thighs Stuffed with Veal and Spinach (page 64).

Italians love game birds of all kinds, especially quail. Pancetta- and Sage-grilled Quail with Wreath of Greens (page 65) is a terrific recipe using them.

Italians have long made use of rabbit and hare. During the Rennaissance, sweet and sour hare was one of the best loved Tuscan dishes. We offer Wine-stewed Rabbit with Chilies (page 65) and Rabbit Ragout with Peppers (page 66).

 *Poultry*

Grilled Chicken Paillards with Sage and Fontina Cheese

2 servings

4 **chicken breast halves, boned**
Salt and freshly ground pepper

5 **teaspoons fresh lemon juice**
3 **teaspoons olive oil**
8 **sage leaves, minced**

2 **ounces Italian Fontina cheese,**
thinly sliced

8 **escarole leaves, white ribs**
removed
Lemon wedges

Pound each chicken breast between 2 sheets of waxed paper to thickness of
⅛ inch. Season each chicken paillard with salt and pepper. Set 1 paillard on
plate. Sprinkle with 1 teaspoon lemon juice and ½ teaspoon olive oil. Press with
¼ of minced sage. Continue layering with remaining paillards, 3 teaspoons
lemon juice, 1½ teaspoons olive oil and sage. Cover stack with waxed paper and
chill 3 hours.

Prepare barbecue (high heat). Set 1 paillard on work surface, sage side up.
Cover with half of cheese. Top with second paillard, sage side down. Press edges
to seal. Repeat with remaining paillards and cheese. Set packets on grill and cook
until chicken is opaque, about 3 minutes on each side.

Meanwhile, mix escarole with remaining 1 teaspoon olive oil. Season with
salt and pepper. Set on grill and cook until wilted and just brown, about 2 minutes on each side.

To serve, divide escarole between plates. Top with chicken. Sprinkle each
with ½ teaspoon of remaining lemon juice. Garnish with lemon.

Chicken Marsala

6 servings

3 **pounds large chicken breast**
halves, skinned and boned

5 **ounces prosciutto**
3 **tablespoons unsalted butter**
2 **tablespoons olive oil**

1 **medium onion, quartered**
8 **ounces small mushrooms, halved**
1 **cup Marsala**
½ **cup whipping cream**

2 **tablespoons minced fresh sage**
leaves or 1½ teaspoons dried,
crumbled
½ **teaspoon salt**

6 **ounces mozzarella cheese, cut into**
1-inch cubes, chilled
5 **ounces Parmesan cheese**
(preferably imported), cut into
1-inch cubes, room temperature

Line baking sheet with waxed paper. Arrange chicken in single layer on sheet.
Freeze chicken until firm but easily pierced through with tip of sharp knife,
about 40 minutes.

Insert ultra thick or thick slicer blade in processor. Stand chicken in feed
tube, wedging tightly. Slice, using firm pressure. Spread in single layer on baking
sheet to thaw. Cut 3 ounces prosciutto into ¼-inch strips. Carefully remove slicer
and insert steel knife. Melt 2 tablespoons butter with oil in heavy large skillet
over medium heat. Pat chicken dry and add to skillet with prosciutto strips.
Cook 1 minute, stirring constantly. Cover and cook until chicken just turns

opaque, about 2 minutes. Transfer to 12-ounce oval gratin dish using slotted spoon. Discard any liquid in skillet.

With machine running, drop onion through feed tube and mince finely. Melt remaining 1 tablespoon butter in same skillet over medium heat. Add onion and mushrooms. Cover and cook until softened, shaking pan occasionally, about 4 minutes. Add Marsala and cook uncovered 1 minute. Transfer mushrooms to chicken mixture using slotted spoon. Add cream, sage and salt to skillet. Simmer until mixture is consistency of whipping cream, about 10 minutes. Remove from heat.

Position rack in center of oven and then preheat to 425°F.

Finely chop both cheeses and remaining 2 ounces prosciutto.

Pour off any liquid from chicken and mushrooms. Add reduced cream sauce to chicken. Top with cheese. Bake until cheese is light brown, about 10 minutes. Serve immediately.

Spicy Chicken with Olives and Anchovies

4 to 6 servings

2 tablespoons (¼ stick) margarine
1 tablespoon olive oil
6 rolled anchovy fillets with capers (reserve 2 teaspoons oil from can)
3 large garlic cloves, pressed
½ teaspoon dried red pepper flakes
1 pound boneless chicken breasts, skinned and cut into 1-inch chunks

¾ cup dry white wine
½ cup small black pitted olives, drained
½ teaspoon dried oregano, crumbled
½ pound freshly cooked spaghetti
Chopped tomatoes

Melt margine with olive and anchovy oils in heavy large skillet over medium-high heat. Add garlic and pepper flakes and cook 1 minute. Add chicken and sauté until lightly browned on all sides, about 5 minutes. Reduce heat to medium. Push chicken to sides of skillet. Place anchovies and capers in center of skillet and mash with back of wooden spoon to make paste. Increase heat to medium-high. Add wine, olives and oregano and stir until chicken is just cooked through, 2 to 3 minutes. Arrange spaghetti on platter and spoon chicken over. Garnish with chopped tomatoes. Serve immediately.

Hunter's Chicken

8 servings

2 ounces dried porcini mushrooms
3 cups chicken stock

¼ cup (or more) olive oil
4 large red bell peppers, cored, seeded and quartered

2 2½-pound chickens, quartered
Salt and freshly ground pepper
1½ pounds sweet Italian sausage, pierced

½ cup (about) dry Marsala

Rinse mushrooms under cold water. Transfer to small bowl. Bring stock to boil. Pour over mushrooms. Let stand 1 hour, stirring occasionally.

Heat ¼ cup oil in heavy large skillet over medium-high heat. Add bell peppers and cook until lightly browned, stirring frequently, about 5 minutes. Remove using slotted spoon.

Pat chicken dry. Sprinkle with salt and pepper. Add to same skillet (*in batches if necessary*) over medium-high heat and brown lightly on all sides, adding more oil to skillet if necessary, about 10 minutes. Remove from skillet. Add sausage and brown well on all sides, about 15 minutes. Remove from skillet; cut into 8 pieces. Pour off fat from skillet; do not wash skillet.

Drain mushrooms, reserving liquid. Strain liquid through several layers of dampened cheesecloth into measuring cup; you should have about 1½ cups. Add enough Marsala to total 2 cups. Stir liquid into same skillet, scraping up browned bits, and bring to boil. Reduce heat and simmer 5 minutes.

Preheat oven to 350°F. Arrange chicken skin side up in single layer in baking dish. Top with bell peppers, sausage and mushrooms. Pour liquid over. Cover tightly. Bake until chicken is tender, basting every 15 minutes, about 1 hour.

Transfer chicken, bell peppers, sausage and mushrooms to platter. Cover and keep warm. Degrease pan juices. Pour into medium saucepan. Boil until liquid is reduced by ⅓, about 15 minutes. Spoon some of liquid over chicken. Pass remainder separately.

Chicken with Tomato, Sweet Fennel Sausage and Polenta

Sweet Italian sausages, with their distinctive fennel taste, add flavor to this dish.

8 servings

1 cup boiling water
1 ounce dried porcini mushrooms

4 pounds chicken legs and thighs
Salt and freshly ground pepper
2 tablespoons (¼ stick) unsalted butter
2 tablespoons olive oil
8 sweet Italian sausages (about 2 pounds)

¼ pound mild coppa,* cut into ¼-inch dice
3 medium leeks (white part only), finely chopped
1 large onion, thinly sliced
1 medium carrot, finely chopped
1 medium celery stalk, finely chopped

4 medium garlic cloves, minced
¾ cup dry Italian red wine (such as Chianti)
2 28-ounce cans Italian plum tomatoes, drained
1½ cups rich chicken or beef stock
⅓ cup tomato paste
2 tablespoons minced fresh basil or 2 teaspoons dried, crumbled
2 teaspoons minced fresh oregano or ½ teaspoon dried, crumbled

Classic Polenta (see page 39)
1 tablespoon minced fresh basil or parsley

Pour water over mushrooms in small bowl. Cover and soak until soft, about 30 minutes. Strain soaking liquid through fine sieve, reserving soaking liquid. Rinse mushrooms; cut out any tough stems and discard.

Pat chicken dry. Sprinkle with salt and pepper. Melt butter with oil in heavy Dutch oven over medium-high heat. Add chicken and brown on all sides. Transfer to plate. Pierce sausages with fork. Add to Dutch oven. Reduce heat to medium and cook until brown on all sides. Add to chicken.

Add coppa to Dutch oven and stir 2 minutes. Add leeks, onion, carrot and celery. Reduce heat to low and cook until vegetables soften, stirring occasionally, about 15 minutes. Add garlic and cook 2 minutes, stirring occasionally. Add wine. Increase heat and boil until almost evaporated. Add mushrooms and soaking liquid, tomatoes, stock and tomato paste. Bring to boil. Add 2 tablespoons basil and oregano. Reduce heat and simmer 15 minutes. Return chicken and sausages to Dutch oven. Simmer until chicken is tender and sausages are cooked through, about 25 minutes. Transfer chicken and sausages to heated plate. Tent with aluminum foil to keep warm.

Boil sauce until thick enough to coat spoon; stirring frequently, about 20 minutes. Season with salt and pepper. Degrease sauce. Spoon polenta onto large platter. Top with chicken and sausage. Spoon some sauce over. Garnish with 1 tablespoon basil. Serve, passing remaining sauce separately.

*Coppa is dried, cured pork shoulder, available at Italian markets.

Stuffed Boneless Chicken with Tarragon Sauce

A spectacular presentation, perfect for buffets and elegant dinners.

10 to 12 servings

Stuffing

1½ pounds ground beef round
½ cup pine nuts, lightly toasted
2 extra-large eggs
2 tablespoons red wine vinegar
2 tablespoons fresh lemon juice
2 garlic cloves, slivered
1 teaspoon grated lemon peel
1 teaspoon freshly ground pepper
½ teaspoon salt
¼ teaspoon freshly grated nutmeg
¼ teaspoon ground cloves
¼ teaspoon cinnamon
¼ teaspoon ground coriander

1 6-pound roasting chicken

½ pound prosciutto, cut into
  ¼ × ¼ × 2-inch strips
½ pound ⅛-inch-thick veal scallops
2 tablespoons fresh lemon juice
1 teaspoon grated lemon peel
½ teaspoon freshly ground pepper
½ teaspoon ground cloves
5 bay leaves
¼ pound thinly sliced ham, cut into
  ¼-inch-wide strips

Orange slices
Bay leaves
Tarragon Sauce*

For stuffing: Mix first 13 ingredients.

To bone chicken: Arrange chicken breast side down on work surface. Cut down back of chicken all the way through to bone from neck to tail, using small sharp knife. Working on one side of backbone, hold blade of knife against bones and scrape meat from carcass with small cuts, gently pulling flesh from carcass with fingers; do not pierce skin. Cut through wing and thigh joints. Continue around carcass to ridge of breast. Repeat on second side of backbone. Lift carcass from flesh and cut against ridge of breastbone to free carcass in one piece. Cut around thigh and leg bones to separate from meat, gently scraping meat from bone down to ¾ inch from end. Using poultry shears, cut leg bones ¾ inch from end and remove bones, leaving end. Scrape meat from first joint of wing bones and pull out bones, leaving second wing bone joint.

Arrange chicken skin side down on work surface. Press some stuffing into wing and leg cavities, then spread half of remaining stuffing over chicken. Insert 1 strip prosciutto into stuffing in each wing and leg cavity. Spread half of remaining prosciutto over stuffing. Cover with veal, then remaining stuffing. Press remaining prosciutto into stuffing. Fold skin in around stuffing. Using thread and trussing needle, sew chicken closed, slightly overlapping edges. Turn breast side up and gently pat to reshape chicken. Sprinkle chicken with 2 tablespoons lemon juice, 1 teaspoon lemon peel, ½ teaspoon pepper and ½ teaspoon cloves. Arrange 5 bay leaves over chicken, then cover with ham strips. Tie drumsticks together at ends. Crisscross string around chicken to hold shape.

Preheat oven to 325°F. Arrange chicken breast side up in greased baking pan. Cook 1 hour, basting occasionally with pan drippings. Cover loosely with foil and continue cooking until golden brown, basting occasionally, about 1¾ hours. Remove chicken from pan. Cool to room temperature. Discard stirring and refrigerate chicken until well chilled, at least 3 hours. (*Can be prepared 3 days ahead.*)

Remove ham and bay leaves from chicken, reserving ham if desired. Cut chicken crosswise into ⅓-inch-thick slices. Arrange on platter. Let stand at room temperature 20 minutes. Garnish with orange slices and bay leaves and serve with Tarragon Sauce.

*Tarragon Sauce

Makes about 2 cups

12 slices white bread (crusts removed), cut into 1-inch pieces
1 cup rich chicken or beef stock or double-strength canned bouillon
¼ cup Sherry vinegar
4 to 5 garlic cloves
4 fresh parsley sprigs, stems removed

1 tablespoon dried tarragon, crumbled
¾ teaspoon freshly ground pepper
Salt

Combine all ingredients except salt in blender. Puree until smooth. Season with salt to taste. (*Can be prepared 1 day ahead and refrigerated. Bring to room temperature before serving.*)

Stuffed Chicken Breasts with Mushroom Cream Sauce

6 servings

12 6-ounce boneless chicken breasts, skinned and trimmed
12 thin prosciutto slices
¾ pound Bel Paese cheese, cut into 12 oblongs
24 asparagus spears, blanched 1 minute and trimmed to 4-inch lengths
¾ pound freshly grated mixed Parmesan and Romano cheese
½ cup minced fresh parsley

Olive oil

All purpose flour
1 pound mushrooms, thinly sliced
¾ cup dry Marsala
6 cups whipping cream
Salt and freshly ground pepper

Pound chicken breasts between sheets of waxed paper to thickness of ¼ inch. Arrange chicken breasts shiny side down. Cover each with 1 prosciutto slice. Set 1 Bel Paese cheese oblong in center of each. Place 2 pieces of asparagus beside cheese. Sprinkle with about 3 tablespoons Parmesan mixture, then parsley. Roll up tightly.

Preheat oven to 350°F. Heat thin layer of oil in heavy large skillet over medium heat. Dredge chicken rolls in flour, shaking off excess. Arrange seam side down in skillet and brown on both sides. Transfer to baking sheet. Pour oil over. Do not wash skillet. Bake chicken until tender, about 15 minutes.

Meanwhile, set skillet over high heat. Add mushrooms and Marsala. Tilt pan, heat wine and ignite. When flames subside, boil until liquid is reduced by half. Add cream to skillet and boil until reduced to saucelike consistency. Season with salt and pepper.

To serve, set 2 chicken rolls on each plate. Spoon Marsala sauce over.

Chicken Galantine Sausage

Chicken skin and prosciutto form the casing for this exceptional sausage.

6 servings

Galantine

1 3¹/₂-pound chicken

³/₄ pound ground pork
1 cup whipping cream
1 ounce minced black truffle
(optional)
Salt and freshly ground pepper

Oil
¹/₄ pound thinly sliced prosciutto

Garlic Sauce

2 tablespoons (¹/₄ stick) unsalted
butter, room temperature
1 scant tablespoon unbleached all
purpose flour

1 medium garlic clove, minced
10 tablespoons lukewarm chicken
broth
1 tablespoon fresh lemon juice
1 scant tablespoon red wine vinegar
Salt and freshly ground pepper
¹/₄ cup olive oil

For galantine: Cut chicken skin down full length of back, using small sharp knife. Separate skin from chicken meat in one piece by gently sliding hand between meat and skin, being careful not to tear skin. Set skin aside.

Remove breast meat from chicken (reserve remaining chicken for another use) and grind in meat grinder, using disc with largest holes. Mix with ground pork, cream, truffle, salt and pepper. To check seasoning, pinch off small piece of stuffing mixture and fry until cooked through. Taste, then adjust seasoning as necessary.

Cut 12 × 18-inch sheet of foil. Brush shiny side with oil. Open chicken skin inside up on work surface. Cover completely with prosciutto. Mound stuffing atop prosciutto in 3-inch-wide strip along 1 long side of chicken skin, leaving 1-inch border. Roll skin up like salami, folding in leg portion of skin and edges. Wrap tightly with prepared foil, oiled side in. Refrigerate at least 30 minutes. (*Can be prepared several hours ahead to this point.*)

Preheat oven to 375°F. Set galantine in baking dish. Bake 1 hour, turning once. Cook while preparing sauce (no longer than 30 minutes).

For sauce: Mix butter, flour and garlic to paste in medium bowl. Blend in broth, lemon juice, vinegar, salt and pepper. Heat oil in heavy small saucepan over low heat. Stir in flour mixture until smooth. Simmer until thick about 10 minutes, stirring frequently.*

Unwrap galantine and cut into 12 slices. Arrange 2 slices on one side of each plate. Spoon sauce into center of plate. Serve immediately.

*For extra flavor sauté two ounces minced black truffle in ¹/₄ cup olive oil over low heat 5 minutes before adding flour mixture.

Rolled Turkey Thighs Stuffed with Veal and Spinach

Any leftover turkey is excellent served cold with homemade mayonnaise.

6 to 8 servings

Veal and Spinach Stuffing
1 pound spinach, stemmed

¼ cup (½ stick) unsalted butter
1 cup finely chopped leek
2 medium shallots, finely chopped
2 medium garlic cloves, minced
1 pound ground veal
½ cup coarse breadcrumbs made from day-old bread
¼ cup freshly grated Parmesan cheese
1 egg
1 tablespoon minced fresh Italian parsley or curly-leaf parsley
1 teaspoon salt
1 teaspoon freshly ground pepper

1 teaspoon fennel seed
½ teaspoon dried thyme, crumbled
¼ teaspoon dried tarragon, crumbled

Turkey
4 14-ounce turkey thighs
Salt and freshly ground pepper
Butter

2 tablespoons (¼ stick) unsalted butter, melted
Italian parsley sprigs

For Stuffing: Rinse spinach. Place in heavy Dutch oven. Cover and cook over high heat until wilted, stirring occasionally, about 2 minutes. Chop coarsely and squeeze dry.

Melt butter in heavy 12-inch skillet over medium heat. Add leek, shallots and garlic. Cook until soft, stirring frequently, about 10 minutes. Transfer to large bowl. Add spinach and all remaining ingredients to bowl. Knead until thoroughly combined. Refrigerate while preparing turkey. (*Stuffing can be prepared 1 day ahead.*)

For turkey: Pat turkey dry. Place 1 thigh skin down on work surface. Cut between bone and meat, using small sharp knife. Remove bone. Cut out ½-inch layer of meat to enlarge pocket left by bone; reserve for another use. Spoon ¼ of stuffing into pocket. Season turkey with salt and pepper. Butter sheet of heavy-duty foil. Arrange stuffed thigh skin side down on foil. Wrap turkey, sealing edges. Repeat with remaining turkey. Arrange foil packages seam side down in heavy roasting pan.

Preheat oven to 350°F. Roast turkey 45 minutes. Open foil and brush turkey with melted butter. Continue cooking until thermometer inserted in center registers 160°F, about 30 minutes. Transfer turkey to plate and let stand 10 minutes. Degrease pan juices. Slice turkey crosswise. Garnish with parsley and serve. Pass pan juices separately.

 Game

Pancetta- and Sage-grilled Quail with Wreath of Greens

12 servings

36 2 × 2 × ¼-inch pancetta* squares
72 2 × 2 × ½-inch French bread squares
24 quail
Olive oil
Salt and freshly ground pepper

6 lemons, quartered
Ground sage
48 large fresh sage leaves

Wreath of Greens**

Cook pancetta in heavy large skillet over medium-high heat until some fat is rendered. Add bread and toss until all of fat is absorbed.

Pat quail dry. Rub generously with oil. Sprinkle with salt and pepper. Squeeze juice of lemon quarter into each quail. Rub inside of each with ground sage. Alternating ingredients, thread 6 bread squares, 4 sage leaves, 3 pancetta squares and 2 quail on each skewer. Repeat with remaining ingredients to make 12 skewers. Cover skewers and refrigerate until ready to grill.

Prepare barbecue with very hot coals. Add soaked mesquite chips if desired. Arrange skewers on grill and cook until quail is golden brown, turning frequently, 10 to 15 minutes. (Watch carefully; bread burns easily.) Transfer kebabs to plates and remove skewers. Surround with some of Wreath of Greens. Serve immediately.

*Italian unsmoked bacon cured in salt, available at Italian markets.

**Wreath of Greens

12 servings

3 medium heads escarole
2 medium heads red leaf or iceberg lettuce
2 bunches arugula

⅔ cup fresh lemon juice
2 tablespoons snipped fresh chives
Salt and freshly ground pepper
2 cups corn oil or vegetable oil

Finely chop escarole, red leaf lettuce and arugula. Combine in large bowl. Blend lemon juice, chives, salt and pepper in small bowl. Whisk in oil in thin stream. Pour over greens and toss.

Wine-stewed Rabbit with Chilies

4 servings

1 5-pound rabbit*
2 tablespoons vegetable oil
2 tablespoons olive oil
3 cups coarsely chopped onion
1 cup dry white wine
Salt and freshly ground pepper
3 medium garlic cloves, crushed
3 small red or green chilies, seeded and thinly sliced crosswise

⅓ cup capers, rinsed and drained
4 thyme sprigs or 2 teaspoons dried, crumbled
2 oregano sprigs or 2 teaspoons dried, crumbled

Discard fat from rabbit. Reserve kidneys and liver. Cut rabbit into 11 serving pieces by cutting rear legs into leg and thigh pieces, loin crosswise into 3 pieces, rib section in half crosswise, leaving front legs whole. Soak in cold salted water to cover 15 minutes. Drain rabbit and pat dry.

Heat both oils in heavy large skillet over medium heat. Add onion and cook until golden brown, stirring frequently, about 8 minutes. Transfer to plate using slotted spoon. Increase heat to medium-high. Add rabbit to skillet in batches (do not crowd) and brown about 5 minutes per side. Transfer to plate. Add wine to skillet, increase heat and boil until reduced to ¼ cup, scraping up any browned bits, about 2 minutes. Return onion and rabbit to skillet. Sprinkle with salt and pepper and turn to coat with juices. Add garlic and chilies. Cover and simmer until rabbit is almost tender when pierced with knife tip, turning occasionally, about 40 minutes.

Meanwhile, remove membrane from kidneys and trim liver. Pat dry. Cut into ⅛-inch dice. Mix into rabbit. Stir in capers, thyme and oregano. Simmer uncovered until kidneys and liver are tender, stirring occasionally, about 6 minutes. (*Can be prepared 1 day ahead and refrigerated. Bring to room temperature, then rewarm in heavy large skillet over medium-low heat, stirring frequently, about 10 minutes.*) Serve immediately.

*If unavailable, two 2½-pound rabbits can be substituted. Cut each into 8 pieces: front legs, hind legs with thighs attached, 2 loin pieces and 2 rib sections.

Rabbit Ragout with Peppers

6 servings

¼ cup (½ stick) butter
2 ounces prosciutto, coarsely chopped
1 4-pound rabbit, rinsed, dried and cut into serving pieces
1 cup beef or chicken broth
4 to 6 parsley sprigs
2 bay leaves
1 rosemary sprig
Salt and freshly ground pepper

¼ cup olive oil
1½ to 2 tablespoons minced garlic
6 anchovy fillets (preferably salt-packed), coarsely chopped
½ cup red wine vinegar
6 large sweet peppers (preferably 3 red and 3 yellow), roasted, peeled, seeded and cut into 2 × ½-inch strips

Melt butter in large skillet over medium-high heat. Add prosciutto and sauté 5 minutes. Add rabbit and brown well on all sides. Stir in broth, parsley, bay leaves, rosemary, salt and pepper. Reduce heat, cover and simmer until rabbit is just fork tender, about 45 minutes to 1 hour. (*Rabbit can be prepared 1 to 2 days ahead to this point, covered and refrigerated. Rewarm slowly over low heat before proceeding.*)

Heat olive oil in small skillet over medium-high heat. Add garlic and sauté until lightly golden. Reduce heat, add anchovy, stirring until dissolved. Increase heat to high, blend in vinegar and boil until vinegar is reduced to 2 to 3 tablespoons. Add to rabbit with peppers. Cover and cook about 20 minutes, removing cover if sauce needs thickening. Serve immediately or remove from heat, cover and rewarm slowly over low heat before serving.

6 ❦ Meat

Although Italians consume most of their meat in the form of cured pork products such as prosciutto, salami, mortadella and coppa, there are still numerous specialties that take advantage of the milky veal of Piedmont and Lombardy, world-class Chianina beef of Tuscany, and succulent lamb of Abruzzi.

Italians tend to prefer white meat to red, i.e., young meat to adult meat—and that means veal. In fact, Italy's veal creations are probably its best-known contribution to the meat course. In this chapter we offer recipes for such time-honored entrées as Saltimbocca ("jump into the mouth") alla Giuliana (page 69), the felicitous marriage of veal scallops and prosciutto; and Traditional Osso Bucco ("bone with a hole") (page 72), veal shank slices with their marrow in an aromatic vegetable sauce, traditionally served with risotto. Some other stand-out dishes include Butterflied Veal Chops with Arugula (page 68), Veal Ragout with Saffron and Tomatoes (page 73) and Frittata-filled Veal Roll (page 70).

There are several famous Italian beef preparations including bresaola (salted, air-dried pressed beef) and carpaccio (marinated slices of raw beef top round), not to mention several of our recipes: Braised Beef Lombard Style (page 75); Neapolitan Steaks (page 73); and Venetian-style Calf's Liver (page 76).

Starting with the abbacchio (suckling lamb) in Rome, the further south you go, the more lamb you will eat, due to the Greek influence and the good grazing lands. Some of our delicious recipes include Lamb with Sweet-Sour Sauce (page 79), Lamb Roast with Pine Nut and Parmesan Crust (page 80) and Herb- and Garlic-marinated Leg of Lamb (page 78).

Not all of Italy's pork goes into cured products, and we offer recipes for Wine-braised Pork Chops with Caramelized Onions (page 76) and Grilled Italian Sausages with Red Onions and Peppers (page 77).

Veal

Butterflied Veal Chops with Arugula

6 servings

6 ½-pound rib veal chops, about ¾ inch thick
6 medium garlic cloves, minced
2 cups dry white wine
1¼ teaspoons salt

4 cups loosely packed arugula leaves (about 2 bunches), coarsely chopped

2 teaspoons extra-virgin olive oil
1 teaspoon red wine vinegar
Freshly ground pepper
Vegetable oil (for deep frying)
3 large eggs, beaten to blend
2 cups fresh white breadcrumbs

Cut 2 inches of chine bone from each chop. Remove fat. Using sharp knife, cut chop lengthwise down center to create two flaps of meat. Spread chop open. Pound meat between sheets of waxed paper to thickness of ⅛ inch. Arrange chops in shallow dish. Spread with garlic. Mix wine and salt. Pour over chops. Let stand at room temperature about 1 hour.

Mix arugula with oil and vinegar. Season with salt and pepper. Set aside. Heat oil in deep fryer to 375°F. Wipe garlic off each chop; pat dry. Dip chops in egg, then coat completely with breadcrumbs, shaking off excess. Fry chops in oil in batches (do not crowd) until golden brown, about 2 minutes. Drain on paper towels. Set chops on plates. Surround with arugula.

Veal Chops Stuffed with Gorgonzola

6 servings

6 1-inch-thick veal loin or rib chops (about 10 ounces each)
¼ pound Gorgonzola cheese
2 tablespoons (¼ stick) butter
2 large garlic cloves, halved
½ cup olive oil
½ cup dry white vermouth

2 shallots, minced
3 fresh sage leaves or ½ teaspoon dried, crumbled
Salt and freshly ground pepper

6 fresh sage leaves

Using sharp knife, cut pocket through center of large muscle in each veal chop; do not cut all the way through. Cream Gorgonzola and butter. Divide among pockets, spreading evenly. Close pockets with small skewers. Rub garlic over both sides of chops. Combine oil, vermouth, shallots, 3 sage leaves, salt and pepper in shallow nonaluminum pan. Add chops and marinate at least 1 hour, turning once; marinade should not seep into pockets.

Preheat broiler. Pat chops dry and arrange on broiler pan. Broil 8 inches from heat source until golden brown and just opaque, basting frequently with marinade, about 6 minutes per side; do not overcook. Remove skewers from chops. Arrange chops on platter. Garnish each with sage leaf.

Saltimbocca alla Giuliana

4 servings

3 tablespoons flour
¼ teaspoon freshly ground white pepper

1 pound well-trimmed veal scallop slices, pounded ¼ inch thick and cut into 1½-inch squares
2 tablespoons olive oil
8 thin slices prosciutto, cut into ½-inch squares

2 tablespoons beef stock
1 tablespoon dry white wine
¼ pound freshly grated Gruyère cheese
2 cups cooked spinach

Combine flour and pepper in bag or pie plate. Dredge veal lightly, shaking off excess. Place large skillet over high heat until very hot, about 30 seconds. Add oil, coating bottom evenly. Add veal and stir-fry until pieces are golden brown, about 2 minutes. Add prosciutto and continue stirring 30 seconds. Add beef stock and wine and stir-fry an additional 30 seconds. Remove from heat and sprinkle with Gruyère. Arrange bed of spinach on heated platter and top with veal mixture. Serve immediately.

Roast Veal with Tomato Sage Relish

A beautiful presentation. The entire dish can be prepared one day ahead.

8 servings

1 3¾-pound boned veal rump roast
½ cup Niçoise olives, pitted and slivered
3 medium garlic cloves, slivered
¼ cup olive oil

Salt and freshly ground pepper
1½ cups chicken stock
1½ cups dry white wine
1 medium lemon, halved

Relish
Olive oil
1 large onion, coarsely chopped or thinly sliced

3 teaspoons minced garlic
2½ pounds tomatoes, peeled, seeded, chopped and well drained
¼ teaspoon salt
Freshly ground white pepper
1 teaspoon minced fresh sage
Sage sprig
Spinach leaves (optional)

Preheat oven to 325°F. Pat veal dry. Pierce deeply all over with small sharp knife. Force olives and garlic into holes. Heat oil in heavy 10- to 12-inch skillet over medium-high heat. Add veal and brown well on all sides.

Transfer veal to rack in roasting pan (reserve drippings in skillet). Season meat with salt and pepper. Combine stock and wine; baste meat with ⅓ cup. Roast 20 minutes. Baste with ⅓ cup more stock mixture and cook 10 minutes. Squeeze juice from half lemon over veal. Continue roasting 30 minutes, basting every 15 minutes with ⅓ cup stock mixture and adding some stock mixture to pan if necessary to keep bottom of pan covered. Squeeze remaining half lemon over veal and cook until thermometer inserted in thickest part of meat registers 150°F, basting occasionally, about 40 minutes. Transfer veal to platter. Boil pan juices until reduced to ¼ cup, scraping up any browned bits. (*Can be prepared 1 day ahead. Cool to room temperature. Store veal and cooking juices separately in refrigerator.*)

For relish: Add enough oil to veal drippings in skillet to measure 3 tablespoons. Heat over medium heat. Add onion and garlic and stir 3 minutes. Gently squeeze tomatoes in kitchen towel to extract as much liquid as possible. Mix tomatoes into skillet. Add veal cooking juices, salt and pepper. Simmer until mixture is thick enough to mound in spoon, stirring occasionally, about 4 minutes. Cool. Mix in minced sage. Transfer relish to bowl. (*Can be prepared 1 day ahead. Cover tightly with plastic and refrigerate.*)

Place relish in center of platter. Garnish with sage sprig. Cut veal into ¼-inch-thick slices. Overlap slices around edge of platter. Garnish platter with clusters of spinach leaves. Serve at room temperature.

Frittata-filled Veal Roll

When the roast is sliced, the filling forms a beautiful spiral pattern.

14 servings

¼ pound pancetta,* minced
2 medium garlic cloves, minced
1 tablespoon olive oil
1 14-ounce head romaine lettuce, shredded
1 small yellow chili, seeded and minced
Salt

5 eggs
2 tablespoons all purpose flour
¼ cup freshly grated Romano cheese
5 tablespoons olive oil

1 6- to 7-pound veal breast, boned and trimmed
Freshly ground pepper

3 tablespoons olive oil
2 tablespoons (¼ stick) butter
2 cups hot milk
Shredded radicchio (optional)

Combine pancetta, garlic and 1 tablespoon oil in heavy large skillet over low heat. Cook until pancetta fat is rendered, stirring occasionally, about 10 minutes. Add romaine, chili and salt. Increase heat to high and stir until romaine is wilted and all moisture has evaporated, about 4 minutes.

Beat 1 egg in large bowl. Sift in flour and beat well. Blend in remaining 4 eggs. Add lettuce mixture, Romano and salt. Heat 4 tablespoons oil in heavy 12-inch omelet pan or skillet over medium heat. Add egg mixture and stir with fork until bottom begins to set, about 3 minutes. Cook without stirring until frittata holds shape, about 4 minutes. Invert onto plate. Add 1 tablespoon oil to skillet. Slide frittata into skillet, uncooked side down. Cook until second side is set, about 3 minutes. Slide onto plate.

Open veal on work surface, cut side up. Cover with waxed paper and pound out to thickness of ½ inch. Sprinkle veal with salt and pepper. Place frittata in center. Roll up jelly roll fashion, starting at short end. Tie veal roll securely with string.

Heat 3 tablespoons oil and butter over medium-high heat in heavy pan just large enough to accommodate veal. Brown veal on all sides, about 15 minutes. Add hot milk. Reduce heat, cover partially and simmer until thermometer inserted in veal registers 150°F, turning occasionally, about 1¾ hours. Let veal rest in juices 20 minutes. Remove string. Slice meat and arrange on radicchio-lined heated platter. Strain and degrease pan juices. Rewarm in heavy saucepan. Serve veal, passing pan juices separately.

*Pancetta, unsmoked bacon cured in salt, is available at Italian markets.

Fennel-stuffed Veal

8 servings

3 small fennel bulbs
(2 pounds total)
6 tablespoons (³/₄ stick) butter
1 small onion, thinly sliced
³/₄ cup beef broth
Salt and freshly ground pepper

1 4-pound boned and butterflied
shoulder of veal
¹/₄ pound thinly sliced prosciutto

1 tablespoon vegetable oil
³/₄ cup finely diced peeled carrot
¹/₂ cup finely diced onion
³/₄ cup dry white wine
1 medium tomato, finely chopped
3 parsley sprigs
1 bay leaf

Discard tough outer layer from fennel; peel away strings. Remove cores of bulbs. Cut each bulb into 8 slices. Melt 4 tablespoons butter in heavy large skillet over medium-low heat. Add onion and cook until translucent, stirring occasionally, about 10 minutes. Add fennel and toss to coat. Add ¹/₄ cup beef broth and season with salt and pepper. Cover and braise until fennel is tender, 20 to 30 minutes. If any liquid remains, uncover and boil until evaporated. Cool mixture completely. (*Can be prepared 3 days ahead and refrigerated.*)

Set veal on work surface exterior side down. Season with salt and pepper. Cover with prosciutto. Spread fennel mixture over. Starting at long side, roll veal up as for jelly roll. Tie with string in several places to secure.

Preheat oven to 350°F. Melt remaining 2 tablespoons butter with oil in Dutch oven or casserole over medium heat. Add veal and brown well on all sides. Remove from pan. Add carrot and onion to pan and stir until lightly browned, about 5 minutes. Add wine, scraping up any browned bits. Boil until liquid is reduced to 3 tablespoons. Add tomato. Return veal to pan. Add remaining broth, parsley and bay leaf and bring to boil. Season with salt and pepper. Cover pan with foil and lid. Transfer to oven and bake until veal is tender, about 1¹/₂ hours.

Remove veal from pan. Let stand 10 minutes. Cut into ¹/₂-inch slices. Serve immediately with pan juices.

Veal Shanks Braised in Red Wine and Garlic

4 servings

2 cups all purpose flour
Salt and freshly ground pepper
4 large center-cut veal shanks
(about 4 pounds total)
¹/₄ cup olive oil

3 leeks, white part only, finely
chopped
1 large onion, finely chopped
1 large carrot, finely chopped
1 bunch Italian parsley, stems and
leaves separated
1 teaspoon dried thyme, crumbled

1 teaspoon dried oregano,
crumbled
1 bay leaf
2 cups veal or chicken stock
1 cup dry red wine

40 large garlic cloves, peeled

¹/₄ cup (¹/₂ stick) unsalted butter,
room temperature, cut into
tablespoons

4 tablespoons grated orange peel

Season flour generously with salt and pepper. Pat veal dry. Dredge in flour, shaking off excess. Heat oil in heavy 4- to 5-quart pot over high heat. Add veal in batches and brown well on all sides, about 15 minutes. Remove veal.

Stir leeks, onion, carrot, parsley stems, thyme, oregano and bay leaf into same pot. Cover and cook over medium-low heat until tender and golden brown, stirring occasionally, about 20 minutes. Add stock and wine and bring to boil. Reduce heat, cover partially and simmer 40 minutes, stirring occasionally to prevent sticking.

Preheat oven to 350°F. Strain vegetable mixture, pressing on solids to extract as much liquid as possible. Return liquid to pot. Add veal and garlic and bring to simmer. Cover and transfer to oven. Bake until veal is tender, turning occasionally, 1½ to 2 hours.

Transfer veal to platter; keep warm. Press liquid and garlic through sieve; you should have 1 to 1½ cups sauce. Return sauce to pot. (If necessary, boil to reduce sauce to required amount.) Set sauce over low heat. Whisk in butter 1 tablespoon at a time.

Mince parsley leaves. Set veal on plates. Spoon sauce over. Sprinkle with parsley and orange peel.

Traditional Osso Bucco

4 servings

4 2-inch-thick veal shank pieces, preferably from meaty part of hind shanks (about 3 pounds total), tied around center
Salt and freshly ground pepper
¼ cup all purpose flour
2 tablespoons (¼ stick) unsalted butter
2 tablespoons vegetable oil or olive oil

1 medium onion, minced
1 medium carrot, finely chopped
1 medium celery stalk, finely chopped
3 thyme sprigs or ¾ teaspoon dried, crumbled
2 parsley sprigs
1 bay leaf

½ cup dry white wine
3 medium garlic cloves, minced
1½ cups brown veal stock or rich chicken stock
1½ pounds ripe tomatoes, peeled, seeded and chopped

1 tablespoon tomato paste

Gremolata
3 tablespoons minced fresh parsley
1 small garlic clove, finely minced
½ teaspoon finely grated lemon peel

Preheat oven to 350°F. Pat veal dry. Sprinkle both sides with salt and pepper. Dredge in flour, patting off excess. Melt butter with oil in heavy large skillet with high sides or Dutch oven over medium-high heat. Add veal and brown on all sides. Transfer to plate.

Reduce heat to low. Add onion, carrot and celery to skillet. Stir until vegetables are tender, scraping up any browned bits, about 5 minutes. Tie thyme, parsley sprigs and bay leaf in cheesecloth. Add to skillet. Mix in wine and garlic. Boil until most of liquid evaporates, stirring constantly. Return veal bone side up to skillet. Add stock and tomatoes. Return to boil. Cover, transfer to oven and bake until veal is very tender when pierced with tip of sharp knife, about 1½ hours, shaking pan occasionally to prevent sticking.

Discard herb bag. Transfer veal to serving platter. Stir tomato paste into sauce. Boil until reduced to about 2 cups, stirring frequently, about 10 minutes. Adjust seasoning. Return veal to skillet. Cover and bring sauce to simmer.

For gremolata: Mix all ingredients.

Sprinkle gremolata evenly over veal and sauce. Cover and simmer 2 minutes. Serve immediately.

Veal Ragout with Saffron and Tomatoes

A rich, aromatic do-ahead stew that is excellent party fare.

12 servings

4 pounds boneless veal shoulder, cut into 2-inch cubes
¼ cup all purpose flour
2 teaspoons salt
Freshly ground pepper
¼ cup (½ stick) butter
⅓ cup vegetable oil
1 Celery Bouquet Garni*

4 cups peeled, seeded and chopped tomatoes

1 large onion, chopped
3 garlic cloves, minced
1 teaspoon saffron threads, crushed
2 cups beef stock (preferably homemade), heated
1 cup dry white wine

Pat veal dry. Combine flour, salt and pepper. Dredge veal in seasoned flour, shaking off excess. Melt butter with oil in heavy large skillet over medium-high heat. Add veal in batches (do not crowd) and brown lightly on all sides. Transfer veal to ovenproof baking dish. Add Celery Bouquet Garni.

Preheat oven to 350°F. Add tomatoes, onion and garlic to skillet, scraping up browned bits. Simmer until onion is transparent, about 10 minutes. Pour over veal. Dissolve saffron in ¼ cup stock. Stir into skillet. Add remaining stock and wine and simmer 5 minutes to blend flavors. Pour over veal. Cover and bake 1½ hours. Uncover and bake until sauce thickens, about 50 minutes. Adjust seasoning. Discard bouquet garni. Serve ragout immediately. (*Can be prepared 3 days ahead. Rewarm gently over low heat.*)

*Celery Bouquet Garni

Makes 1

1 celery stalk, cut into 3-inch lengths
1 fresh parsley sprig

1 fresh thyme sprig
1 fresh rosemary sprig
1 bay leaf

Using kitchen twine, tie celery pieces around herb sprigs and bay leaf.

 *Beef*

Neapolitan Steaks

8 servings

⅓ cup (about) extra-virgin olive oil
12 ounces mushrooms, trimmed and thinly sliced
6 ounces prosciutto, coarsely chopped

⅓ cup coarsely chopped Italian parsley
8 1-inch-thick beef fillets
2 tablespoons fresh lemon juice
Salt and freshly ground pepper

Preheat oven to 500°F. Grease baking dish with 2 tablespoons oil. Spread mushrooms, prosciutto and parsley in dish. Drizzle enough oil over to coat. Arrange steaks in single layer atop bed of mushrooms, spacing ¾ inch apart. Brush steaks with oil. Bake 8 minutes. Turn steaks. Sprinkle with lemon juice, salt and pepper. Continue cooking to desired degree of doneness, about 3½ minutes for medium-rare. Let rest 5 minutes before serving.

Beef Stew with Chick-Peas, Garlic and Zucchini

4 servings

³/₄ cup dried chick-peas (garbanzo
beans),* rinsed and sorted
6 cups cold water

3 tablespoons vegetable oil
2 pounds boneless beef chuck,
trimmed, patted dry and cut into
1¹/₄- to 1¹/₂-inch pieces
1 large onion, chopped
1 tablespoon plus 1 teaspoon
all purpose flour

2¹/₄ pounds tomatoes, peeled, seeded
and chopped

1³/₄ to 2¹/₄ cups beef stock
2 tablespoons minced garlic
1 tablespoon minced fresh
rosemary or 1 teaspoon dried,
crumbled
1 serrano chili, seeded and minced
Salt
1 tablespoon tomato paste

1 pound zucchini, cut into
¹/₂-inch pieces

Soak chick-peas in 3 cups cold water 8 hours or overnight. Drain; rinse under
cold water and drain again. Transfer to medium saucepan and cover with 3 cups
cold water. Bring to boil. Cover, reduce heat to low and simmer until tender,
about 1¹/₄ hours. Set aside.

Position rack in lower third of oven and preheat to 450°F. Heat oil in heavy
4- to 5-quart flameproof casserole over medium-high heat. Add ¹/₃ of beef and
brown on all sides, making sure pieces do not touch, 6 to 7 minutes. Transfer
beef to plate using slotted spoon. Repeat with remaining beef. Add onion to pan,
reduce heat to low and cook until translucent, stirring often, about 7 minutes.
Return beef to pan; reserve any juices on plate. Sprinkle beef with flour. Toss
gently until well coated. Transfer to oven and bake uncovered, stirring once,
5 minutes. Remove from oven.

Reduce oven temperature to 325°F. Pour reserved juices from plate over beef.
Add tomatoes and enough stock to barely cover. Add garlic, rosemary, chili and
salt. Bring mixture to boil on top of stove, scraping down any browned bits from
sides and bottom of pan. Transfer to oven, cover and bake, stirring occasionally,
1 hour. Add more stock if mixture appears dry or sauce is too thick. Stir tomato
paste into stew. Drain chick-peas and mix into stew. Continue baking until beef
is tender when pierced with tip of sharp knife, 30 to 45 minutes.

Transfer stew to top of stove and uncover. Sauce should be thick enough to
lightly coat back of spoon. If sauce is too thick, stir in additional stock. If sauce is
too thin, carefully remove beef and vegetables using slotted spoon and boil sauce,
stirring often, until slightly thickened. Return beef and vegetables to sauce. (*Can
be prepared 3 days ahead, covered and refrigerated or 1 month ahead and frozen.*)
Add zucchini and simmer until tender, about 5 minutes. Adjust seasoning. Serve
Beef Stew hot.

*If desired, 1¹/₂ cups rinsed, canned chick-peas can be used. Do not soak or cook.

Braised Beef Lombard Style

Beef is larded with carrots and pancetta for a delicious taste. The beans are a nice accompaniment.

6 to 8 servings

6 medium carrots, peeled and soaked in cold water 30 minutes
8 ounces pancetta* or fatty prosciutto, coarsely chopped
½ cup olive oil
Freshly ground pepper

1 3-pound beef rump roast, trimmed

2 medium-size red onions, coarsely chopped
3 medium celery stalks, chopped
4 ounces prosciutto, chopped
1 cup dry red wine
4 juniper berries
2 bay leaves
2 whole cloves

1 teaspoon dried thyme
1 teaspoon dried marjoram

1 cup fresh Italian plum tomatoes, quartered or 1 cup canned, drained
1 cup (about) warm beef stock (optional)

Boiled Italian Beans**
Bay leaves

Drain 2 carrots and chop finely. Marinate with half of pancetta, ¼ cup oil and pepper in small bowl 30 minutes.

Puncture meat 2 inches deep in 10 places, using small sharp knife or larding needle. Enlarge holes with fingers. Drain carrot mixture, reserving oil. Stuff mixture into holes. Tie meat securely with twine to hold shape.

Drain remaining 4 carrots and chop coarsely. Heat reserved oil and remaining ¼ cup oil over medium heat in heavy casserole just large enough to hold meat. Stir in carrrots and remaining 4 ounces pancetta, onions, celery and prosciutto and sauté 5 minutes. Pat beef dry and add to pan. Cover and brown on all sides, about 20 minutes. Pour in wine. Wrap juniper berries, 2 bay leaves, cloves, thyme and marjoram in cheesecloth. Add to meat. Cover and simmer 20 minutes.

Puree tomatoes through food mill into pan. Pour in enough broth to cover ⅔ of meat with liquid. Cover and simmer gently until meat is tender when pierced with knife, turning occasionally, about 1½ hours, adding more broth if necessary to keep ⅔ of meat covered with liquid.

Remove meat from casserole. Degrease cooking juices. Set pan over high heat and boil until liquid is reduced to 4 cups, about 10 minutes. Discard twine and cut meat into ¾-inch slices. Overlap down center of platter. Spoon sauce around meat. Arrange beans around sauce. Garnish with bay leaves.

*Italian-style unsmoked bacon, preserved in salt. Available at Italian markets.

**Boiled Italian Beans

Makes about 6 cups

2 cups dried cannellini beans or lentils
Water
6 cups cold water

1 tablespoon olive oil
1 medium garlic clove, minced
Coarse salt

Cover beans with cold water and soak overnight at room temperature.

Drain beans well. Combine with 6 cups cold water in heavy large saucepan. Add oil, garlic and salt and bring to boil. Reduce heat, cover and simmer until beans are tender, about 2 hours. Serve hot. (*Can be prepared 1 day ahead and refrigerated. Rewarm before serving.*)

Venetian-style Calf's Liver

*Serve this appealing dish
with rice to absorb the
delicious sauce.*

4 servings

2 tablespoons (¼ stick) butter
1 medium onion, sliced

1 cup sliced mushrooms

24 ounces ¼-inch-thick slices calf's
liver, cut into 3 × ½-inch strips
All purpose flour
½ cup (1 stick) unsalted butter
¼ cup olive oil

¾ cup demi-glace or beef stock
¼ cup dry white wine
4 teaspoons minced fresh parsley
Salt and freshly ground pepper

Melt 1 tablespoon butter in heavy large skillet over medium-low heat. Add onion
and cook until tender, stirring frequently, 8 minutes. Transfer onion to plate.

Add 1 tablespoon butter to same skillet and melt over medium-high heat.
Add mushrooms and cook until tender, stirring frequently, about 4 minutes. Add
to onions.

Lightly coat liver with flour. Melt ½ cup butter with oil in another heavy
large skillet over high heat. Add liver and cook about 1 minute on each side for
medium-rare. Transfer liver to heated platter using slotted spoon. Add onion and
mushrooms to skillet. Stir over medium-high heat 1 minute. Add demi-glace or
stock, wine and parsley. Boil until mixture coats back of spoon, scraping up any
browned bits, about 1 minute for demi-glace or 6 minutes for stock. Season with
salt and pepper. Return liver to skillet and stir until heated through. Serve hot.

 *Pork*

Wine-braised Pork Chops with Caramelized Onions

*Veal chops can replace the
pork chops; just cook them
a little less.*

*2 servings; can be doubled
or tripled*

2 1¼-inch-thick pork loin chops
1¼ teaspoons minced fresh rosemary
1¼ teaspoons minced fresh sage
1 small garlic clove, minced
Salt and freshly ground pepper
2 tablespoons (¼ stick) butter
1½ teaspoons olive oil
All purpose flour

1 large onion, sliced
⅓ cup dry white wine
1 cup unsalted beef broth

2 teaspoons snipped fresh chives
1 teaspoon grated orange peel
Preserved lingonberries*

Pat pork dry. Combine 1 teaspoon rosemary, 1 teaspoon sage, garlic, salt and
pepper; press into chops. Melt ½ tablespoon butter with oil in heavy medium
skillet over medium-high heat. Dredge pork in flour. Add to skillet and cook
until brown, about 2 minutes per side. Transfer to plate.

Pour off fat in skillet and wipe out any burned bits. Add 1½ tablespoons
butter to skillet and melt over medium-high heat. Add onion and cook until
brown and almost tender, stirring frequently, about 9 minutes. Blend in wine and
boil until reduced to glaze, scraping up any browned bits, about 1 minute. Mix in
broth and ¼ teaspoon each rosemary and sage and bring to boil. Return pork to
skillet with any juices on plate. Reduce heat, cover and simmer until pork is

cooked through, turning and basting occasionally, about 15 minutes. Transfer pork chops to heated serving plates.

Boil pan juices and onion until liquid coats spoon, about 3½ minutes. Spoon onion mixture over chops. Combine chives and orange peel. Sprinkle over pork. Garnish plates with lingonberries. Serve immediately.

*Available at specialty foods stores.

Arista alla Fiorentina

4 to 6 servings

1 3½- to 4-pound loin of pork, boned (reserve bones)
1 fresh green or red chili, halved, seeded and deveined
1 tablespoon fresh rosemary
1 tablespoon fresh thyme
Salt and freshly ground pepper
1 medium to large head of garlic (about 12 cloves), separated and peeled
4 fresh basil sprigs

1 bunch Italian parsley (about 1½ cups chopped)
6 tablespoons olive oil

2 tablespoons olive oil
3 celery stalks, coarsely chopped
1 medium onion, coarsely chopped
1 medium carrot, coarsely chopped
6 tablespoons water
4 cups dry white wine
3¼ cups water

Rub loin with chili, rosemary and thyme. Sprinkle with salt and pepper. Using long, thin knife, make lengthwise slit through meat. Combine garlic, basil and parsley on work surface and chop finely. Transfer to small bowl. Add 6 tablespoons olive oil and blend well. Fill roast with mixture.

Preheat oven to 350°F. Chop reserved bones. Arrange in roasting pan. Set loin over bones. Rub loin with 2 tablespoons olive oil. Roast 45 minutes. Turn loin over. Add celery, onion and carrot to pan. Pour in 6 tablespoons water and continue roasting until thermometer inserted in thickest part of meat registers 175°F to 180°F, about 45 minutes. Transfer loin to heated platter, set aside and keep warm. Add wine to roasting pan. Place over medium-high heat and bring to boil. Let boil 2 minutes. Reduce heat, add remaining water and boil gently 45 to 55 minutes (sauce will be thin).

Slice loin and arrange on platter. Strain sauce and degrease as necessary. Spoon some of sauce over. Pass remainder separately.

Grilled Italian Sausages with Red Onions and Peppers

Wrap a loaf of Italian bread in foil and heat on the edge of the grill as the sausages cook. Extra grilled sausage, peppers and onions can be added to cooked rice for a piquant salad.

4 to 6 servings

2 pounds sweet Italian sausage (preferably in 1 large coil)
1½ pounds hot Italian sausage (preferably in 1 large coil)

Vegetable oil
2 red onions, peeled and cut into ⅜-inch-thick slices

½ cup (about) olive oil
3 red bell peppers, cut into 1½-inch triangles
3 rosemary sprigs, soaked in cold water 1 hour and drained

Pierce sausages all over with fork. Bring water to boil in base of steamer set over medium-high heat. Arrange sausages on steamer rack. Cover tightly and cook until firm and opaque, turning halfway through steaming, 10 to 15 minutes, depending on thickness. Cool on paper towels. (*Can be prepared up to 1 day ahead and refrigerated. Bring sausage to room temperature before continuing.*)

Prepare barbecue grill with white coals. Brush hinged grill rack with vegetable oil. Arrange onions in center of rack. Brush with olive oil. Close rack and place on grill. Cook until onions are brown on both sides, brushing with olive oil before turning. Transfer to warm platter and tent with foil. Repeat with peppers, then sausages, adding rosemary sprigs to coals 3 minutes before sausages are finished.

 Lamb

Herb- and Garlic-marinated Leg of Lamb

6 to 8 servings

1 cup olive oil
1 onion, sliced
⅓ cup dry white wine
⅓ cup fresh lemon juice
⅓ cup chopped fresh parsley
3 garlic cloves, minced
1½ tablespoons dried rosemary, crumbled

2 teaspoons Dijon mustard
½ teaspoon salt
½ teaspoon freshly ground pepper
¼ teaspoon dried red pepper flakes
1 5- to 6-pound leg of lamb, boned, butterflied and trimmed

Combine first 11 ingredients. Place lamb in large roasting pan. Pour marinade over. Cover lamb and refrigerate overnight, turning at least once.

Prepare barbecue grill with hot coals. Place lamb on grill and cook 15 minutes per side for rare, basting occasionally with marinade. Let stand 10 minutes before slicing and serving.

Lamb Rotolo with Leek-Basil Stuffing and Red Wine Sauce

8 servings

3 tablespoons unsalted butter
2½ cups chopped leek (white part only)
2 medium garlic cloves, minced
¾ cup minced fresh basil
Salt and freshly ground pepper

1 6½-pound leg of lamb, boned and butterflied
Olive oil

1 cup water
1 large carrot, sliced
1 large onion, chopped

1½ cups dry red wine
4 tablespoons (½ stick) unsalted butter, room temperature

Melt 3 tablespoons butter in heavy large skillet over medium heat. Add leek and garlic and stir until wilted and most of liquid evaporates, about 5 minutes. Mix in basil. Season with salt and pepper. Cool completely.

Preheat oven to 450°F. Trim fat on outside of lamb to thin layer. Arrange lamb cut side up on surface. Cut out any sinews and pieces of fat. Cut shallow incisions in thick parts of meat and open to form even surface. Spread leek mixture over lamb, leaving 1-inch border. Roll lamb up, tucking in ends. Tie with string at 1-inch intervals to hold shape. Arrange seam side down on rack in roasting pan. Rub top and sides with oil and sprinkle with salt and pepper. Pour 1 cup water into pan. Add carrot and onion. Place lamb in oven and reduce heat to 350°F. Roast until thermometer inserted in center registers 135°F for medium-rare, about 1 hour and 20 minutes.

Transfer lamb to heated platter and tent with foil. Degrease pan drippings. Add wine to roasting pan. Bring to boil, scraping up any browned bits. Strain liquid through fine sieve into heavy small saucepan, pressing on solids to extract as much liquid as possible. Boil liquid until reduced to ¾ cup. Cool slightly. Whisk in 4 tablespoons butter 1 tablespoon at a time. Remove foil. Slice lamb across grain and remove string. Arrange on platter. Top with sauce and serve.

Lamb with Sweet-Sour Sauce

A variation of a traditional Italian method of preparing wild boar.

6 servings

2 garlic cloves, minced
1 tablespoon dried rosemary, crumbled
1 teaspoon crushed juniper berries
1 clove, crushed
Salt and freshly ground pepper
1 6-pound crown roast of lamb or 3 2-pound racks of lamb
3 cups red wine
1 cup red wine vinegar

Olive oil

Sauce
2 tablespoons unsweetened cocoa powder
1½ tablespoons sugar
2 tablespoons minced pine nuts
2 tablespoons minced pitted prunes
2 tablespoons minced golden raisins
2 to 3 strips orange peel

Combine garlic, rosemary, juniper berries, clove, salt and pepper in small bowl. Cut small slits between ribs of lamb and fill with garlic mixture. Transfer lamb to large plastic bag. Mix wine and vinegar in medium bowl and pour over lamb. Seal bag tightly. Marinate lamb in refrigerator for 24 hours, turning occasionally to redistribute liquid.

Preheat oven to 325°F. Pour enough olive oil into roasting pan to cover bottom. Drain lamb, reserving marinade. Pat meat dry and transfer to roasting pan. Roast lamb until tender and thermometer inserted in thickest part of meat without touching bone registers 140°F, about 25 minutes.

For sauce: Strain marinade into medium saucepan. Add cocoa and sugar and stir until dissolved. Add pine nuts, prunes, raisins and orange peel. Place over medium heat and bring to simmer. Cook until liquid is reduced by half. Strain sauce again and set aside.

Transfer lamb to warm serving platter and tent with foil. Skim fat from pan juices. Add juices to sauce. Return mixture to medium heat and simmer, stirring, until heated through. Adjust seasonings. Slice lamb and top each serving with 3 tablespoons of sauce.

Lamb Roast with Pine Nut and Parmesan Crust

6 servings

½ cup pine nuts (2½ ounces), toasted
2 ounces Parmesan cheese (preferably imported), cut into 2 pieces
1 slice soft white bread (with crust), torn into pieces
2 teaspoons Dijon mustard
1 large garlic clove

½ teaspoon dried rosemary, crumbled
¼ teaspoon salt
Freshly ground pepper
1 egg white

1 3½-pound leg of lamb (sirloin end), boned and trimmed
Salt

Position rack in center of oven and preheat to 450°F. Oil roasting pan.

Combine pine nuts, cheese, bread, mustard, garlic, rosemary, ¼ teaspoon salt and pepper in processor. Blend in egg white using 3 to 4 on/off turns.

Season underside of lamb with salt and pepper. Arrange seasoned side down in prepared pan. Using spatula, spread nut mixture over top of lamb, pressing gently to adhere. (*Can be prepared 1 day ahead, covered tightly and refrigerated. Bring to room temperature before continuing.*) Roast lamb 15 minutes. Reduce temperature to 375°F and continue cooking to desired doneness, or about 15 more minutes for rare (thermometer inserted in thickest part of lamb will register 125°F; cook longer for medium rare or well done). Let stand 10 to 15 minutes. Carve lamb into thin slices and serve.

Rack of Lamb in Gorgonzola Sauce

4 servings

1½ cups fresh breadcrumbs
½ teaspoon dried rosemary, crumbled
½ teaspoon dried basil, crumbled
½ teaspoon dried sage, crumbled
Salt and freshly ground pepper
2 racks of lamb (16 ribs), room temperature
Dijon mustard

3 jumbo egg yolks, room temperature

2 ounces Gorgonzola cheese, room temperature
1½ tablespoons fresh lemon juice
½ teaspoon cornstarch
¼ teaspoon salt
1 cup (2 sticks) unsalted butter, melted
¼ cup whipping cream, room temperature

Preheat oven to 400°F. Mix breadcrumbs, herbs, salt and pepper in processor. Rub lamb generously with mustard. Coat with breadcrumb mixture, pressing to adhere. Arrange racks in roasting pan. Roast until outside is crisp but inside is still pink, 20 to 25 minutes; do not overcook.

Blend yolks, cheese, lemon juice, cornstarch and ¼ teaspoon salt in processor until smooth. With machine running, add butter through feed tube in thin stream. With machine running, add cream through feed tube in thin stream. Transfer to saucepan and keep warm in tepid water bath.

Cut racks into ribs. Arrange 4 ribs on each plate. Spoon sauce over. Serve immediately.

7 ❦ *Vegetables and Salads*

The quality of Italian produce is matchless, so it's not surprising that vegetables are the backbone of Italian cooking. They appear as appetizers, in soups, mixed with pasta, as main dishes, side dishes and in-between dishes. No matter how they are prepared, they are always treated with respect and usually served on their own plate. Indeed, in summer, many Italians live almost exclusively on fresh vegetables.

The ancient Romans were devoted producers and consumers of vegetables, a talent they inherited from their predecessors, the Etruscans, who passed on the arts of irrigation, pruning and rotation of crops. The Romans did them proud as they went on to develop new varieties of vegetables (such as broccoli and cabbage) and to perfect old ones.

The colonization of the Americas brought sweet and hot peppers, beans, squash, corn and cornmeal, tomatoes and other basics of Italian cooking to the Mediterranean area in the sixteenth century. It was a period of great creativity in Italian gastronomy, and cooks were able to make optimum use of these new ingredients.

Some of Italy's best-loved vegetables are represented in our assortment of recipes. There are Peas with Rosemary and Toasted Pine Nuts (page 85), Baked Onions with Red Wine Vinegar (page 84), Stuffed Tomatoes Baked in Tomato Sauce (page 87) and Abruzzi Vegetable Casserole (page 88).

In a typical Italian dinner, if vegetables are being served with it, a simple salad of greens tossed in olive oil and lemon juice or vinegar with salt will accompany the meal. However, if the salad is the only vegetable being served, then it becomes more elaborate with the addition of other vegetables for color, texture and flavor. Some of our salad recipes include Fresh Mushroom and Artichoke Salad (page 90), Istrian Tomato Salad (page 90) and Panzanella Bread Salad (page 92).

Vegetables

Broccoli di Rapa with Prosciutto

If broccoli di rapa, an Italian green, is unavailable, use turnip greens, beet greens, dandelion greens or spinach.

4 to 6 servings

2 pounds broccoli di rapa, stems peeled, tough outer leaves discarded

6 ounces prosciutto, sliced ⅛ inch thick

¼ cup olive oil

2 small red or green chilies, seeded (ribs discarded), thinly sliced crosswise

Salt and freshly ground pepper
Olive oil
Lemon wedges

Cut broccoli di rapa into 3 pieces crosswise. Blanch in large pot of boiling salted water 2 minutes. Rinse with cold water, drain and pat dry.

Separate prosciutto into meat and fat. Cut into ⅛-inch dice. Heat prosciutto fat and ¼ cup oil in heavy large skillet over low heat until fat is rendered and pieces are crisp and brown, about 10 minutes. Remove browned pieces with slotted spoon and reserve. Mix in broccoli, prosciutto meat, chilies, salt and pepper. Cover and cook until greens are tender, 8 to 15 minutes, adding water occasionally 2 tablespoons at a time if too dry. Add prosciutto fat and toss well. Serve hot or at room temperature. Pass olive oil and lemon wedges separately.

Cabbage with "Little" Sauce

4 servings

Prosciutto Sauce
½ pound prosciutto, sliced ¼ inch thick
2 tablespoons vegetable oil
1 cup tomato puree
½ cup dry white wine
¼ cup minced fresh Italian parsley
2 tablespoons minced fresh oregano or 2 teaspoons dried, crumbled
½ small red or green chili, seeded and thinly sliced or ½ teaspoon dried red pepper flakes
Salt

3 tablespoons olive oil
1 tablespoon vegetable oil
1 medium onion, coarsely chopped
1 1½-pound savoy cabbage, trimmed and cut into ¾-inch-wide wedges
1 cup water (or more)
Salt and freshly ground pepper

For sauce: Trim fat from prosciutto and cut into ⅛-inch dice. Cut meat into ¼-inch dice. Heat 2 tablespoons vegetable oil in heavy medium skillet over low heat. Add prosciutto fat and cook until rendered, stirring occasionally, about 10 minutes. Discard any unmelted fat, using slotted spoon. Mix in tomato puree, prosciutto meat, wine, parsley, oregano, chili and salt. Simmer until oil separates, stirring occasionally, about 30 minutes.

Meanwhile, heat olive oil and 1 tablespoon vegetable oil in heavy large skillet over medium-low heat. Add onion and cook until translucent, stirring frequently, about 6 minutes. Add cabbage and stir to coat with oil. Add 1 cup water, salt and pepper and bring to boil. Reduce heat, cover and simmer until cabbage is tender, adding more water if cabbage sticks, about 25 minutes. Uncover, increase heat and boil until liquid evaporates, stirring constantly. Mix in sauce and serve.

Cauliflower Cornucopias

Use these colorful cauliflower "bowls" as centerpieces on a buffet.

12 servings

2 large heads cauliflower (about 3 pounds each), green leaves intact
6 tablespoons fresh lemon juice
2 tablespoons salt

4 cups thinly sliced carrots (about 8), steamed to crisp-tender
4 cups trimmed brussels sprouts (about 1½ pounds), steamed to crisp-tender
3 cups thinly sliced radishes (about 20 large)
2 cups snow peas, trimmed and halved on bias if large (about 5 ounces)

1⅓ cups (about 6 ounces) Niçoise olives, pitted
1 cup sliced green onions
⅔ cup minced fresh parsley
¼ cup white wine vinegar
2 tablespoons Dijon mustard
1 tablespoon minced fresh oregano or 1 teaspoon dried, crumbled
1½ teaspoons salt
2 garlic cloves, halved
Freshly ground pepper
⅔ cup olive oil

Combine cauliflower, lemon juice and 2 tablespoons salt in large bowl. Add water to cover. Let stand 1 hour.

Drain cauliflower. Divide into 1½-inch florets, leaving leaf shells intact. Set aside 4 cups florets; reserve remainder for another use. Remove as much inner core as possible from each leaf shell. Slice bottom of cores so shells stand upright. Combine shells with enough ice water to cover.

Steam cauliflower florets until crisp-tender. Mix florets, carrots, brussels sprouts, radishes, snow peas, olives, onions and parsley in large bowl. Blend vinegar, mustard, oregano, 1½ teaspoons salt, garlic and pepper in another bowl. Whisk in olive oil in thin stream. Pour dressing over vegetables and toss well. Cover and refrigerate at leat 2 hours. Adjust seasoning. (*Can be prepared 2 days ahead. Do not add radishes until 2 hours before serving.*)

Drain cauliflower shells; dry. Fill with vegetables. Serve at room temperature.

Braised Fennel, Carrots and Snow Peas

6 servings

3 medium fennel bulbs, tough outer layer discarded, strings peeled, trimmed
4 medium carrots (8 ounces total), peeled
¼ pound snow peas, stringed and halved

¼ cup (½ stick) unsalted butter
½ to ¾ cup chicken stock
Salt and freshly ground pepper

Halve fennel lengthwise and discard core. Cut crosswise into ¼-inch-thick slices. Cut carrots diagonally into ¼-inch-thick slices. Blanch snow peas in large pot of boiling salted water until just tender, about 2 minutes. Drain and pat dry.

(*Can be prepared 1 day ahead. Wrap vegetables in damp towel and plastic bag and refrigerate.*)

Melt butter in heavy large skillet over medium-high heat. Add fennel and carrots and stir until coated with butter. Add ½ cup stock and bring to simmer. Reduce heat to low. Cover and cook until vegetables are tender, stirring occasionally and adding remaining ¼ cup stock if all liquid evaporates, 10 to 12 minutes. Uncover and boil to evaporate liquid if necessary. Add snow peas and stir until heated through, about 1 minute. Season with salt and pepper. Serve immediately.

Italian Green Bean Salad

6 servings

2 pounds green beans, trimmed

Mustard Vinaigrette
3 tablespoons balsamic vinegar
1 tablespoon stone-ground mustard
1 teaspoon salt
9 tablespoons olive oil

1 large red onion, peeled, halved and thinly sliced
1 cup pine nuts, toasted
Salt and freshly ground pepper

1 large head radicchio
1 large head Bibb lettuce

Cook beans in 2 quarts boiling salted water until crisp-tender, about 7 minutes. Drain. Rinse under cold water and drain well. Pat dry.

For vinaigrette: Combine vinegar, mustard and salt in medium bowl. Slowly whisk in oil in thin stream.

Combine beans, onion and ½ cup pine nuts in large bowl. Mix in vinaigrette. Season with salt and pepper. Let marinate 15 to 30 minutes.

Alternate radicchio and Bibb lettuce leaves over large platter. Mound bean mixture in center. Sprinkle with remaining ½ cup pine nuts and serve.

Baked Onions with Red Wine Vinegar

Perfect with the Neapolitan Steaks (see page 73).

8 servings

4 large yellow onions
4 large red onions
Salt and freshly ground pepper

½ cup olive oil
6 tablespoons wine vinegar

Preheat oven to 350°F. Oil ovenproof baking pan large enough to accommodate onions in single layer. Remove papery outside skin from onions, leaving most of peel on. Quarter onions through root end. Place in prepared pan. Sprinkle with salt and pepper. Pour oil over; turn to coat. Cover tightly with foil. Bake 30 minutes. Uncover and continue baking until onions are tender, turning occasionally, 20 to 30 minutes. Transfer onions to platter. Add vinegar to baking dish. Bring to boil, scraping up any browned bits. Pour over onions. Let steep at least 1 hour, turning occasionally. Serve at room temperature.

Glazed Baby Onions

8 servings

40 pearl onions
1 cup dry white wine
¹/₂ cup beef broth
Salt and freshly ground pepper

2 teaspoons sugar
¹/₄ cup (¹/₂ stick) butter, diced
3 tablespoons minced fresh parsley

Cook onions in large amount of boiling water 1 minute. Refresh under cold water until cool enough to handle. Drain. Peel and trim. Cut small cross in root ends. Transfer to heavy large skillet. Add wine and broth. Season with salt and pepper. Sprinkle with sugar. Dot with butter. Bring to boil. Reduce heat, cover and simmer until onions are tender, about 40 minutes. If liquid remains in skillet, uncover and boil until reduced to glaze. (*Can be prepared 3 days ahead. Cool completely, cover and refrigerate. Reheat gently before serving.*) Toss with parsley.

Peas with Rosemary and Toasted Pine Nuts

6 servings

¹/₂ cup chicken stock
2 green onions (white part and 2 inches of green part), cut into ¹/₂-inch pieces
¹/₂ teaspoon sugar
3 pounds fresh peas, shelled*

6 large Boston lettuce leaves
3 tablespoons butter

10 tablespoons pine nuts
1 tablespoon minced fresh rosemary or 1 teaspoon dried, crumbled
Salt and freshly ground pepper

Bring stock, green onions and sugar to simmer in medium saucepan. Add peas. Simmer until just tender, 5 to 10 minutes. Drain, discarding liquid. (*Can be prepared 1 day ahead. Spread on kitchen towel and cool. Refrigerate.*)

Arrange lettuce on platter. Melt butter in heavy large skillet over medium heat. Add pine nuts and stir until golden, 2 to 3 minutes. Mix in rosemary and cook 1 minute. Add peas and green onions and stir until hot. Season with salt and pepper. Spoon mixture into lettuce leaves and serve.

*If unavailable, two 10-ounce packages frozen peas can be substituted. Thaw; cook with green onions for about 3 minutes in stock. Continue as above.

Peppers with Almonds

14 servings

5 tablespoons olive oil
1 cup slivered almonds
2¹/₂ pounds red bell peppers, cut into ¹/₂-inch-wide strips
1¹/₂ pounds green bell peppers, cut into ¹/₂-inch-wide strips

6 tablespoons red wine vinegar
¹/₄ cup sugar
Salt
1 to 2 tablespoons warm water

Heat oil in heavy large skillet over medium-low heat. Add almonds and stir until light brown, about 5 minutes. Add peppers, vinegar, sugar and salt. Mix to coat peppers well. Increase heat to medium-high. Cover and cook 10 minutes, stirring occasionally. Uncover and continue cooking until peppers are tender, stirring occasionally and adding water if peppers begin to stick, about 7 minutes. Serve warm or at room temperature.

Genoa-style Spinach

4 to 6 servings

2 pounds fresh spinach, stemmed, cooked and drained
⅓ cup seedless golden raisins plumped in white wine and drained
¼ cup toasted pine nuts
Pinch of freshly grated nutmeg

¼ cup olive oil
2 tablespoons chopped fresh parsley
4 anchovy fillets, drained and cut into small pieces
Salt and freshly ground pepper

Combine spinach, raisins, pine nuts and nutmeg in medium bowl.

Heat olive oil in large saucepan over medium heat. Add parsley and anchovies, reduce heat to low and stir until anchovies are dissolved. Stir in spinach mixture, cover and cook over very low heat about 5 minutes. Season with salt and pepper. Transfer to serving dish and serve immediately.

Swiss Chard and Vegetable Nest

6 servings

½ pound Swiss chard, preferably red-stemmed

2 tablespoons olive oil
1 cup diced peeled carrot
1 cup diced red onion

1 cup diced cooked unpeeled red-skinned potatoes
Salt and freshly ground pepper

Cut out stems from chard leaves and thinly slice. Cut leaves into julienne.

Heat oil in heavy large skillet over medium heat. Add chard stems and onion and stir 2 minutes. Add potatoes and cook until vegetables are crisp-tender, stirring occasionally, about 5 minutes. Season with salt and pepper.

Meanwhile, bring large pot of salted water to boil. Add chard leaves and return to boil. Drain well. Season chard generously with salt and pepper.

Mound sautéed vegetables on platter. Surround with chard leaves.

Slow-simmered Tomatoes with Herbs

The long cooking of the tomatoes brings out a full, rich flavor. Serve with crusty bread to soak up the sauce.

8 servings

8 medium tomatoes
¼ cup olive oil
Pinch of sugar
Salt and freshly ground pepper

½ cup extra-virgin olive oil
2 medium garlic cloves, minced

½ cup minced fresh parsley
½ cup minced fresh basil
2 tablespoons minced fresh mint

Cut small slice from tomatoes on end opposite stem. Pour ¼ cup oil into heavy skillet just large enough to accommodate tomatoes in single layer. Place over medium-low heat. Add tomatoes cut side down and cook 15 minutes. Sprinkle with sugar, salt and pepper. Turn tomatoes. Reduce heat to low and cook 2½ hours.

Heat ½ cup extra-virgin olive oil and garlic in heavy small skillet over low heat. Add herbs, salt and pepper. Cook 8 minutes, stirring occasionally. Transfer tomatoes to platter. Pour herb mixture over and serve.

Stuffed Tomatoes Baked in Tomato Sauce

6 servings

6 large tomatoes
Coarse salt

1 cup fresh breadcrumbs, toasted
¾ cup freshly grated Parmesan cheese (preferably imported)
4 extra-large eggs
6 tablespoons olive oil
6 fresh basil leaves, torn into pieces
2 teaspoons grated lemon peel
Pinch of grated orange peel
Salt and freshly ground pepper
Freshly grated nutmeg

1 pound fresh Italian plum tomatoes, quartered, or 1 pound canned, drained
6 fresh mint leaves
6 fresh basil sprigs

Soak 6 tomatoes in cold water to cover for 10 minutes. Drain. Cut off top third of tomatoes and reserve. Scoop out seeds using melon baller; pour off juice (do not break up pulp). Sprinkle cavities with coarse salt. Drain tomatoes 5 minutes. Rinse and pat dry. Arrange in 8¾ × 13½-inch baking dish.

Mix breadcrumbs, Parmesan, eggs, 2 tablespoons oil, basil, lemon peel, orange peel, salt, pepper and nutmeg in large bowl. Fill each tomato ⅔ full with mixture. Cover with tops.

Preheat oven to 375°F. Puree 1 pound tomatoes through fine disc of food mill into medium bowl. Mix in remaining 4 tablespoons oil, mint, salt and pepper. Pour around tomatoes. Add water to dish so liquid comes ⅓ up sides of tomatoes. Bake until just tender, about 20 minutes. Transfer to plates. Boil cooking liquid until reduced to saucelike consistency if necessary. Spoon around tomatoes. Garnish with basil. Serve warm or cold.

Sautéed Zucchini Rounds

8 servings

3 pounds small zucchini, cut into ⅓-inch-thick rounds
Salt

3 tablespoons butter
2 tablespoons vegetable oil

3 leeks (white part only), minced
1 small onion, minced
3 tablespoons balsamic or red wine vinegar

Toss zucchini with salt in colander. Top with plate and weight. Let stand 1 hour to drain. Rinse; dry well.

Melt butter with oil in heavy large skillet over medium-low heat. Add leeks and onion and cook until softened, stirring occasionally, about 10 minutes; do not brown. (*Can be prepared 8 hours ahead.*) Add zucchini. Season with salt. Increase heat to high. Sauté 3 minutes. Stir in vinegar and let boil until reduced to glaze. Serve immediately.

Deep-fried Zucchini and Eggplant in Rosemary Batter

4 to 6 servings

1½ cups warm water
⅓ cup yellow cornmeal
1¼ cups unbleached all purpose flour
2 tablespoons minced fresh rosemary
Pinch of salt

6 quarts water
2 tablespoons salt
1 pound eggplant, trimmed and cut lengthwise into quarters, then sliced crosswise into ½-inch pieces

⅔ pound zucchini, trimmed and sliced into ¼-inch rounds

5 cups vegetable oil
Coarse kosher salt

Slowly whisk 1½ cups water into cornmeal in medium bowl. Sift in flour, whisking constantly. Stir in rosemary and salt. Let batter stand 20 minutes.

Bring 6 quarts water to boil. Stir in 2 tablespoons salt. Add eggplant and zucchini and return to boil. Stir vegetables 1 minute. Drain; plunge immediately into ice water. Let cool completely. Drain; dry on paper towels.

Heat oil in deep fryer or heavy large saucepan to 375°F. Dip vegetables in batter, allowing excess to drip back into bowl. Lower into oil in batches (do not crowd) and cook until crisp and golden brown, about 2 minutes. Remove using slotted spoon and drain on paper towels. Sprinkle with coarse salt. Serve deep-fried vegetables immediately.

Abruzzi Vegetable Casserole

8 servings

3 parsley sprigs
1 medium carrot
1 medium celery stalk
1 large garlic clove
½ teaspoon fresh oregano or ¼ teaspoon dried, crumbled
Salt and freshly ground pepper

Olive oil
3 medium onions, thinly sliced

3 medium-size red or green bell peppers, cut into ¼-inch strips
3 medium boiling potatoes, peeled and cut into ⅛-inch rounds, soaked in cold water until ready to use
3 medium zucchini, cut into ⅛-inch rounds
¼ cup olive oil

Finely chop parsley, carrot, celery, garlic and oregano in processor using on/off turns. Season with salt and pepper.

Preheat oven to 350°F. Generously oil 2-quart baking dish. Layer remaining vegetables in dish, sprinkling chopped vegetable mixture between layers and drizzling with olive oil as necessary. Drizzle top with olive oil. Bake until vegetables are tender, 45 to 60 minutes. Pour off excess oil. Serve casserole warm.

Irwin Horowitz

Top: Coco-Amaretto Delight
Bottom: Tartufi

Irwin Horowitz

Clockwise from left: Frittata-Filled Veal Roll; Peppers with Almonds; Brigands' Pasta; Cherry Ricotta Cake

Victor Scocozza

Clockwise from right center: Fennel-Stuffed Veal with Glazed Baby Onions; Shrimp and Vegetable Salad; Polenta Appetizers; Sautéed Zucchini Rounds; Candy-Shaped-Pasta Pie

Victor Scocozza

Zabaglione Cake with Chocolate Frosting

Brian Leatart

Opposite, clockwise from top:
Swiss Chard and Vegetable Nest;
Veal Chops Stuffed with Gorgonzola;
Risotto with Shrimp, Mussels and
Peas; Strawberry Panini

Left: Pumpkin Turkey Anolini with Sage Butter; right: Gnocchi Roll Florentine Style

Brian Leatart

 Salads

Festive Salad

A refreshing party salad any time of year. Use whatever greens are in season.

20 servings

Salad

Tender inner leaves of one head of lettuce, torn into bite-size pieces

1 each red, yellow and green bell pepper, seeded and cut into bite-size pieces

2 carrots, shredded

2 small cucumbers, unpeeled, cut into bite-size pieces

1 large red onion, slivered

3 to 4 ounces each rughetta,* chicory and red-leaf lettuce, torn into bite-size pieces

Mustard Anchovy Dressing

4 2-ounce cans anchovy fillets (about 30), drained

1 7½-ounce jar cocktail onions (about 30), drained

3 tablespoons Dijon mustard

2 cups olive oil

1¼ cups wine vinegar
Freshly ground white pepper

1 cup halved pitted black olives

For salad: Combine all ingredients in large glass salad bowl and set aside.

For dressing: Combine anchovies, onions and mustard in processor and mix until smooth. Add oil and vinegar and blend 5 seconds. Season with pepper to taste. Pour over greens and toss well. Top with black olives and serve.

*Available in specialty produce markets.

Romaine and Grapefruit Salad with Toasted Pine Nuts

Toasting the pine nuts adds a pleasant nuance to this refreshing salad. The grapefruit juice-enhanced dressing can be prepared one day ahead.

2 servings

1 large grapefruit

3 tablespoons olive oil

1 tablespoon minced fresh parsley

1 teaspoon fresh lemon juice
Salt and freshly ground pepper

3 cups romaine leaves, rinsed, dried and torn into pieces

½ green bell pepper, cored, seeded and cut into fine julienne

2 tablespoons toasted pine nuts

Peel and section grapefruit over small bowl to catch juice; reserve sections. Combine 1 tablespoon juice with oil, parsley, lemon juice, salt and pepper to taste and whisk to blend.

Combine grapefruit sections, romaine and green pepper in large bowl. Add dressing and toss gently. Divide between salad plates. Sprinkle with pine nuts and serve immediately.

Istrian Tomato Salad

6 servings

3 large ripe tomatoes, each cut into
4 rounds
Salt and freshly ground pepper
4 hard-cooked eggs, each cut on
diagonal into 3 slices
3 ounces pimientos, drained and
coarsely chopped
1 ounce anchovies, coarsely
chopped

1 green onion, minced
1 small garlic clove, minced
½ teaspoon fresh lemon juice
1 small red onion, minced
6 tablespoons olive oil
2 tablespoons red wine vinegar
⅓ cup minced fresh parsley

Arrange tomato rounds on platter. Sprinkle with salt and pepper. Top each round with egg slice. Combine pimientos, anchovies, green onion, garlic and lemon juice. Divide mixture among egg slices. Sprinkle with red onion. Whisk oil and vinegar. Season with salt and pepper. Pour over tomatoes. Garnish with parsley.

Fresh Mushroom and Artichoke Salad

12 servings

4 large artichokes
½ lemon

¾ pound mushrooms, thinly sliced
5 ounces Parmesan cheese, shaved
with potato peeler (about 2 cups)

1 cup olive oil
⅓ cup lemon juice
Salt and freshly ground pepper
Butter lettuce leaves (garnish)

Snap off upper ¾ of each artichoke leaf (leaving just inner cone of leaves), rubbing exposed parts with lemon as you work to prevent discoloration. Cut off cone of leaves to just above artichoke bottom. Trim and discard darker green parts using paring knife (leave heart and choke intact). Bring large amount of salted water to rapid boil in large pot (*or prepare steamer*). Squeeze juice of cut lemon into water, then add lemon shell. Add artichokes, cover pot with paper towel and boil or steam until just crisp-tender, about 3 minutes. Drain well; pat dry. Cool.

To serve, remove chokes with spoon or knife tip, then slice artichoke bottoms thinly. Transfer to large bowl. Add mushrooms and cheese. Whisk olive oil into lemon juice 1 drop at a time. Pour dressing over mushroom mixture and toss gently. Season with salt and pepper to taste. Line individual plates with lettuce. Top evenly with salad.

Pepper, Mushroom and Parmesan Salad with Garlic Dressing

6 servings

½ cup olive oil
¼ cup red wine vinegar
1 teaspoon minced garlic
¼ teaspoon salt
Freshly ground pepper

3 medium red bell peppers,
cut into julienne
1 medium green bell pepper,
cut into julienne
1 pound mushrooms, sliced

2 cups sliced celery
1 large red onion, thinly sliced
1 cup coarsely grated imported
Parmesan cheese
¼ cup chopped fresh parsley
Additional coarsely grated
imported Parmesan cheese

Combine first 5 ingredients in jar. Cover and shake to blend.

Combine all remaining ingredients except additional Parmesan in shallow bowl. Toss gently to mix. Add dressing and toss well. Divide salad among plates. Pass additional Parmesan.

Shrimp and Vegetable Salad

Accompany this salad with breadsticks for a crisp counterpoint.

8 servings

¼ cup minced fresh parsley
2 tablespoons minced red onion
1 tablespoon (or more) fresh lemon juice
1 tablespoon Dijon mustard
1 egg yolk
1 teaspoon anchovy paste
½ cup olive oil
2 tablespoons capers, rinsed and drained
Salt

5 red bell peppers
40 medium shrimp, peeled, deveined and cooked
½ pound green beans, trimmed and blanched until tender

Lettuce leaves
¾ cup fresh or frozen peas, blanched until tender

Blend parsley, onion, 1 tablespoon lemon juice, mustard, yolk, and anchovy paste in bowl. Whisk in oil in thin stream. Stir in capers. Adjust seasoning with salt and more lemon juice. (*Can be prepared 2 days ahead and refrigerated.*)

Char peppers over gas flame or in broiler until blackened on all sides. Wrap in paper bag and let steam 10 minutes. Peel and seed. Rinse if necessary; pat dry. Cut each pepper into 8 strips. (*Can be prepared 1 day ahead and refrigerated.*)

Toss shrimp and green beans *separately* with enough dressing to coat. Cover and refrigerate for 1 hour.

Line salad plates with lettuce leaves. Alternate 5 bell pepper strips and small bundles of green beans in pinwheel fashion around each plate. Arrange 5 shrimp in center of pinwheel. Sprinkle with peas. Drizzle with dressing. Serve immediately.

Salad of Zucchini, Yellow Squash and Romaine with Rosemary Vinaigrette

8 servings

1½ pounds small zucchini, cut into 2 × ¼-inch julienne
1½ pounds small yellow crookneck squash, cut into 2 × ¼-inch julienne

Vinaigrette
2 tablespoons plus ¾ teaspoon balsamic vinegar

1½ teaspoons Dijon mustard
¾ teaspoon salt
9 tablespoons plus 1½ teaspoons olive oil
1 teaspoon minced fresh rosemary

1 large head romaine lettuce
Freshly ground pepper

Blanch zucchini and yellow squash in large pot of boiling water until just crisp-tender, about 1½ minutes. Drain. Rinse with cold water and drain well. Pat dry. (*Can be prepared 6 hours ahead. Wrap vegetables in kitchen towel and refrigerate.*)

For vinaigrette: Combine vinegar, mustard and salt in bowl. Slowly whisk in oil in thin stream. Stir in rosemary.

Set aside large outer romaine leaves for garnish. Cut out tough center stems from remaining romaine; cut leaves into 2 × ½-inch strips. Mix zucchini, yellow squash and ½ cup vinaigrette in large bowl. Let marinate 10 minutes. Mix in romaine strips and enough vinaigrette to coat. Season with salt and pepper. Line shallow bowl with reserved romaine leaves. Mound salad in center and serve.

Panzanella Bread Salad

8 servings

1 1-pound loaf very stale Italian Country Bread (see page 45) or French bread, cut into ½-inch cubes
1 cup olive oil
⅓ cup white wine vinegar
2 tomatoes, cored, seeded and coarsely chopped
2 hard-cooked eggs, chopped
1 cucumber, peeled, seeded and coarsely chopped
1 onion, finely chopped

1 carrot, thinly sliced
1 celery stalk, thinly sliced
3 anchovy fillets, chopped
2 tablespoons chopped fresh basil (or more)
1 generous tablespoon capers
Chopped fresh mint leaves
Salt and freshly ground pepper

Place bread cubes in large bowl. Add enough cold water to cover. Let stand 30 minutes. Drain bread well; squeeze dry and fluff with fingers. Transfer to large serving bowl. Add remaining ingredients and toss thoroughly. Adjust seasoning. Chill until ready to serve.

8 ❧ Desserts

The average Italian family eating at home usually ends its meal with fruit and cheese. And why not? Italy boasts orchards and orchards of fruit trees up and down the peninsula, wild berries in the woods, and tropical fruits in the south. And Italy's cheesemakers from Lombardy to Sicily are busy making such delicacies as Parmesan, Romano, Gorgonzola, Bel Paese and mozzarella.

Italians tend to indulge in sweets away from the dining table, in the midmorning or late afternoon at pastry shops, ice cream parlors or cafes. It's there that the country's pastry chefs produce some of the most spectacular and delicious desserts in all of Europe. Their work is rarely done in restaurant kitchens and practically never duplicated in the home, except for special occasions or holidays.

Italians have an impressive store of desserts, developed through the centuries and passed along to other countries in Europe. The wide array of prepared desserts include elaborate pastries, ice creams, creams, custards, soufflés, frozen molded desserts, sweet breads, nut biscuits, specialties made with chestnuts and from chestnut flour, crepes, rice desserts, fruit fried in batter, meringues, poached and stuffed fruits and fruits wrapped in pastry.

Some of the desserts represented in our collection include Zuccotto (page 103), a Florentine frozen dessert; Fried Zeppole (page 113), a Neapolitan fritter; Hazelnut Semifreddo (page 100), a chilled pudding; Cherry Ricotta Cake (page 105); Zabaglione Cake with Chocolate Frosting (page 107); Frozen Amaretto Soufflé (page 99); and Peach and Frangelico Gratin (page 96).

Oranges in Marsala

6 servings

4 large navel oranges
1 cup dry Marsala
¼ cup sugar
6 whole cloves

2 3-inch cinnamon sticks
1 vanilla bean, split
¼ cup raisins

Using sharp knife, peel oranges, removing all white part. Cut crosswise into ¼-inch-thick slices. Place in glass bowl. Cook Marsala, sugar, cloves, cinnamon and vanilla in heavy medium saucepan over low heat, swirling pan occasionally, until sugar dissolves. Increase heat and boil until reduced by half, about 12 minutes. Stir in raisins. Pour mixture over oranges. Cover and refrigerate at least 2 hours or overnight. Discard cloves, cinnamon and vanilla before serving.

Zuppa di Frutta

6 servings

2 cups well-chilled whipping cream
5 tablespoons plus 1 teaspoon sugar
2 tablespoons grappa* or brandy
1 large peach, halved and cut into 12 slices
1 large plum, halved and cut into 12 slices

1 large nectarine, halved and cut into 12 slices
6 large strawberries, hulled and halved
3 dozen blueberries

Whisk cream, sugar and grappa in large bowl to blend. Pour into six shallow bowls. Divide fruit evenly among bowls. Serve immediately.

*Italian spirit distilled from the grape skins, pulp and seeds that remain after the juice is pressed out. Available at liquor stores.

Little Crosses

Marmalade and walnut-stuffed figs, assembled in the shape of a cross.

Makes 8

¼ cup (½ stick) unsalted butter, room temperature
3 tablespoons powdered sugar
¼ cup orange marmalade
1 tablespoon minced candied citron or 1 teaspoon finely grated lemon peel

32 Calimyrna figs
32 walnut halves

2 tablespoons powdered sugar
1 teaspoon cinnamon

Grease baking dish with ¼ cup butter. Sift 3 tablespoons sugar over butter. Mix marmalade and citron. Cut figs in half, without cutting through stems. Arrange cut side up on surface. Spread cut side of 2 figs with marmalade mixture. Form cross by arranging 1 fig atop the other, cut side up, overlapping at stem end only. Set walnut atop each fig half. Top each fig with another, cut side down. Repeat with remaining figs, marmalade and nuts. Transfer to prepared dish. (*Figs can be prepared 6 hours ahead.*)

Preheat oven to 350°F. Combine 2 tablespoons sugar and cinnamon and sift over figs. Bake until figs are hot, about 10 minutes. Serve warm.

🍎 *Italian Cheeses*

Cheeses are a fundamental ingredient in Italian cooking as well as an integral part of a typical Italian meal. An assortment of cheeses and fruit is a classic way to end a meal. Accompanied by a full-bodied red wine and a crusty loaf of bread, cheeses can be the perfect finale for any meal from the simple to the elaborate.

Bel Paese—A delicate flavor and rich buttery texture make this ivory-colored cheese both excellent in cooking and in serving as a table cheese. With a name that translates to "beautiful country," nothing less should be expected.

Fontina—This soft, delicately flavored cow's milk cheese is a classic in Italian cooking, yet equally appropriate as a dessert cheese. Round, wheel-shaped in form, it should be white to straw yellow in color.

Gorgonzola—This is Italy's entry into the "blue" cheese category. Considered mild for this type, it is softer and more spreadable than France's Roquefort. It is excellent as a dessert cheese served with pears and apples, and its pungent flavor adds zip to many classic recipes.

Mascarpone—A fresh, snow-white double-cream cheese that is mild in taste, with a texture of thick whipped cream, this is often served for dessert simply sprinkled with powdered chocolate or with liqueurs. It can also substitute for butter or cream in pasta sauces.

Mozzarella—Fresh Italian "wet" mozzarella, saturated with its own whey, is made from either cow's milk or more classically from the milk of the water buffalo. It is delicious seasoned simply with salt and pepper and a dressing of olive oil, but it is more commonly known as a cheese used in cooking—its mellow accent enhances the flavor of other ingredients.

Parmesan—As king of Italian cheeses, good imported Parmesan cannot be compared to the pre-grated product found on supermarket shelves. It is a fundamental ingredient in cooking yet an excellent table cheese as well. The cheese should be light straw yellow in color and have a granular texture with a moist, rich, barely salty flavor.

Provolone—Mild, Sharp and Smoked are the three "flavors" that you may find in an Italian cheese shop. Most often made from cow's milk, provolone can also be found made from the milk of water buffalo. Its mildly piquant flavor makes it an excellent table cheese, especially when accompanied by a robust Italian red wine.

Ricotta—Not really a cheese but rather a byproduct of cheesemaking, specifically mozzarella, ricotta is soft, white and spoonable with a light milky flavor. It is a common ingredient found in pasta, rice and dessert recipes.

Romano—Made from whole sheep's milk, this white-and-grayish cheese has a sharp piquant flavor. Like Parmesan, it is a classic dessert cheese served with fruit and also grates well to be used in cooking.

Peach and Frangelico Gratin

2 servings

¾ pound ripe peaches, peeled, pitted
and thinly sliced
2½ tablespoons sugar
1 tablespoon Frangelico liqueur
1½ teaspoons fresh lemon juice

¼ cup (½ stick) unsalted butter
½ cup fresh coarse white
breadcrumbs
½ cup finely ground toasted
hazelnuts

Combine peaches, 1½ tablespoons sugar, Frangelico and lemon juice. Divide between 2 small gratin dishes.

Preheat oven to 400°F. Melt butter in heavy small saucepan. Remove from heat. Stir in remaining 1 tablespoon sugar, breadcrumbs and hazelnuts. Sprinkle over peaches. Bake until bubbly and browned, about 15 minutes. Serve warm or at room temperature.

Mascarpone with Amaretto Sauce

*Serve with amaretti or
other biscotti.*

6 servings

6 egg yolks
9 tablespoons sugar
4 tablespoons amaretto liqueur

¾ pound mascarpone cheese,* room
temperature

¼ cup sour cream
1½ tablespoons amaretti (Italian
macaroon) crumbs

Whisk yolks and sugar in heavy medium saucepan until thick and pale yellow. Set pan over larger pan of gently simmering water. Whisk in 2 tablespoons amaretto and stir 30 seconds. Add remaining amaretto and whisk until slowly dissolving ribbon forms when whisk is lifted, about 3 minutes. Remove pan from over water. Immediately dip pan into ice water and whisk sauce to cool slightly. Refrigerate until well chilled, 3 to 4 hours.

Using wooden spoon, cream mascarpone in large bowl. Blend in sour cream. Transfer to pastry bag fitted with large star tip. Pipe decoratively into goblets. Beat sauce until smooth. Spoon over cheese. Top with crumbs.

*If unavailable, blend ¾ pound cream cheese with 6 tablespoons whipping cream and ¼ cup sour cream.

Rice Pudding with Candied Orange Peel

12 to 16 servings

5½ cups milk
1 cup Arborio rice*

½ cup orange honey
½ cup sugar
6 eggs
1 cup candied orange peel, finely
diced
½ cup plus 3 tablespoons butter,
melted

1 teaspoon orange flower water

½ cup whipped cream
Freshly grated nutmeg
Candied orange peel

Combine milk and rice in heavy-bottomed large saucepan over medium-high heat. Cover and bring to boil. Reduce heat and simmer until rice absorbs milk and mixture is thickened, about 30 to 35 minutes, stirring occasionally and watching carefully so rice does not burn. Remove pan cover and let rice cool 10 minutes.

Preheat oven to 350°F. Butter 9 × 13 × 2½-inch oval ceramic baking dish. Transfer rice to processor and mix to coarse puree (do not overmix; rice should retain some texture). Blend honey, sugar and eggs in large bowl. Stir in rice. Gently fold in orange peel, butter and orange flower water. Pour into prepared dish. Set dish in larger pan. Pour hot water into pan to come ⅔ up sides of baking dish. Bake until set, about 45 minutes. Let cool.

Whip cream in small bowl until just stiff. Transfer to pastry bag fitted with star tip. Pipe 12 to 16 evenly spaced rosettes over top of pudding. Sprinkle rosettes with small amount of nutmeg, then candied orange peel. Serve rice pudding at room temperature.

*Long-grain rice can be substituted. Rinse in fine-mesh strainer under cold water before cooking as described for Arborio rice.

Coco-Amaretto Delight

6 servings

Coconut-Chocolate Crust
2 cups sweetened flaked coconut

6 ounces semisweet chocolate chips
2 tablespoons (¼ stick) unsalted butter
1 tablespoon light corn syrup

Chocolate Cigars (garnish)
6 ounces semisweet chocolate chips

Almond Filling
¼ cup Amaretto liqueur
2 teaspoons unflavored gelatin

½ cup sour cream, room temperature
1½ cups whipping cream
1 cup powdered sugar
¾ cup lightly toasted finely ground almonds
Chopped toasted almonds (optional garnish)

For crust: Lightly grease 9- to 10-inch pie plate or deep square serving dish. Place coconut in medium bowl and warm in 150°F oven.

Combine chocolate chips, butter and corn syrup in top of double boiler over hot (not simmering) water. Stir until melted and smooth. Pour chocolate over warmed coconut and mix with 2 forks until thoroughly blended. Press coconut mixture evenly into bottom and sides of pie plate or dish. Chill.

For chocolate cigars: Melt chocolate in top of double boiler over hot water, stirring until smooth. Spread chocolate over back of baking sheet into 4 × 6-inch rectangle. Cool to room temperature (65°F to 70°F) or refrigerate to firm, but chocolate must be room temperature to shape. Using cheese-shaver server (wire cheese cutter will not work), start an inch from short end of chocolate and pull server toward you in slightly upward motion so that chocolate will curl up and around. Use fingers to aid curling if necessary. Wrap cigars in plastic and refrigerate.

For filling: Combine ¼ cup liqueur with gelatin in small heat-resistant cup and mix until softened. Place cup in simmering water and heat until gelatin is completely liquefied, about 2 to 3 minutes. Transfer gelatin to large bowl. Add sour cream, blending well. Stir in cream and powdered sugar. Whip until stiff. Fold in almonds and spoon into shell. Decorate with chocolate cigars and chopped toasted almonds, if desired. Refrigerate until set, at least 2 hours.

Sweet Cappuccino Cream

4 servings

4 egg whites
¼ cup sugar
2 teaspoons distilled white vinegar
½ cup well-chilled whipping cream
2 egg yolks
2 tablespoons firmly packed light brown sugar
1½ teaspoons instant espresso powder dissolved in 1 teaspoon hot water

1 teaspoon cinnamon
1 teaspoon brandy (optional)
Pinch of salt

¼ cup pine nuts, toasted

Combine egg whites and ¼ cup sugar in food processor and mix 8 seconds. With machine running, pour vinegar through feed tube and blend until whites are stiff and hold shape, about 2 minutes, 20 seconds. Using spatula, gently transfer to medium bowl. (Do not clean work bowl.) With machine running, pour cream through feed tube and process until thick, about 1 minute; do not overprocess. Transfer cream to small bowl. Add yolks, brown sugar, dissolved espresso, cinnamon, brandy (if desired) and salt to work bowl and blend until fluffy, about 1 minute. Spoon whites and cream in circle atop mixture and blend using 2 on/off turns. Run spatula around inside of work bowl. Blend just until whites are incorporated, using about 2 on/off turns (some streaks of white may remain; do not overprocess mixture).

Spoon ⅓ cup cappuccino cream into each of 4 parfait glasses. Sprinkle each with 1½ teaspoons pine nuts. Top with remaining cream. Garnish each with 1½ teaspoons pine nuts. Cover tightly and freeze until firm. (*Can be prepared 1 week ahead.*) Let stand in refrigerator 1 hour before serving.

Tartufi

Can be prepared one month ahead.

10 servings

1 cup superfine sugar
⅔ cup Dutch process cocoa
2 teaspoons instant espresso powder
⅓ cup water

4 egg yolks

10 maraschino cherries, stemmed, pitted, rinsed, drained and soaked in 2 tablespoons rum

1 cup whipping cream
⅔ cup coarsely chopped semisweet chocolate
⅓ cup chopped toasted almonds

Chopped or shaved chocolate (garnish)

Sift sugar, cocoa and espresso into heavy medium saucepan. Whisk in water. Place over medium heat and bring to boil. Cook, stirring constantly, until all sugar is dissolved and mixture is smooth, about 10 minutes.

Beat egg yolks with electric mixer on high speed in large bowl until light and fluffy. Reduce speed to medium, add hot chocolate mixture in slow steady stream and continue beating until cool, stopping once to scrape down sides and bottom of bowl. Chill 1 hour.

Remove maraschino cherries from rum using slotted spoon and set aside to drain. Mix rum into cooled chocolate.

Whip cream in medium mixing bowl until stiff peaks form. Stir 1 large spoonful of whipped cream into chocolate mixture to loosen, blending well.

Gently fold in remaining cream, ²/₃ cup coarsely chopped semisweet chocolate and chopped toasted almonds. (Be careful not to deflate whipped cream.)

Arrange 10 decorative foil-lined paper cups in muffin pan.* Fill each cup ¹/₃ full with chocolate mixture. Arrange cherry in center and fill to ²/₃ full. Sprinkle lightly with chopped or shaved chocolate and freeze at least 4 hours. (*If freezing longer, cover with plastic and foil.*) Serve directly from freezer.

*Can also be spooned into individual cups.

Frozen Amaretto Soufflé

8 servings

Butter
Sugar

1¹/₂ cups sugar
6 eggs, room temperature
6 egg yolks, room temperature

3 tablespoons amaretto liqueur
3 cups whipping cream

Fresh fruit and mint sprigs
(garnish)

Prepare collar for 2-quart soufflé dish by cutting strip of foil long enough to wrap around dish with some overlap. Fold in half lengthwise. Generously butter one side and sprinkle with sugar. Wrap around dish, buttered side in, letting foil extend 3¹/₂ inches above rim. Secure tightly with string.

Add 1¹/₂ cups sugar, eggs and yolks to top of double boiler set over warm (not hot) water over low heat and stir constantly with whisk or rubber spatula until just warm, about 12 minutes. Transfer egg mixture to large bowl of electric mixer and beat until stiff, about 10 minutes. Blend in amaretto. Whip cream in another large bowl until soft peaks form. Gently fold cream into egg mixture, blending well. Pour soufflé into prepared dish. Freeze until firm and set, at least 5 hours.

To serve, let soufflé soften in refrigerator 15 minutes. Spoon soufflé onto individual plates. Garnish with fresh fruit and mint sprigs.

Meringue with Italian Cherry Ice Cream

8 servings

Italian Cherry Ice Cream
2 eggs, separated, room temperature
10 amarene cherries in syrup,*
quartered and pitted,
1 tablespoon syrup reserved
¹/₂ teaspoon vanilla
1 cup whipping cream, well chilled
Pinch of cream of tartar
¹/₄ cup sugar

Meringue
2 egg whites, room temperature
Pinch of cream of tartar
¹/₂ cup sugar

Whipped cream
Amarene cherries, drained

For ice cream: Blend yolks, 1 tablespoon reserved syrup and vanilla in small bowl. Whip cream to soft peaks in chilled bowl. Fold in yolk mixture. Beat whites with cream of tartar until soft peaks form. Add sugar 1 tablespoon at a time, beating until mixture is stiff but not dry. Gently fold whites into cream. Fold in cherries. Transfer to ice cream maker and freeze according to manufacturer's instructions. Turn into container. Cover and freeze several hours, or overnight, to mellow.

For meringue: Preheat oven to 200°F. Grease baking sheet and dust with flour. Draw 8-inch diameter and 6-inch diameter rounds on sheet. Beat whites with cream of tartar until soft peaks form. Add sugar 1 tablespoon at a time, beating until stiff and shiny. Transfer meringue to pastry bag fitted with medium star tip. Pipe mixture in concentric circles to cover both rounds. Bake until meringues are dry and do not stick to baking sheet, about 4 hours. Transfer to racks and cool.

To assemble: Let ice cream soften slightly in refrigerator. Place large meringue round on platter. Smooth ice cream atop meringue, spreading to edge. Top with small meringue circle. (*Can be prepared 1 day ahead and frozen. Soften at room temperature 5 minutes before serving.*) Just before serving, decorate with whipped cream and cherries.

*Amarene cherries are available at Italian markets and specialty foods stores.

Quick Tortoni

12 servings

1 **quart vanilla ice cream, slightly softened**
½ **cup dry macaroon crumbs**
¼ **cup chopped candied cherries**

¼ **cup mini semisweet chocolate chips**
1 **tablespoon brandy**
½ **cup whipping cream, whipped**

Place paper liners in muffin tin. Combine first 4 ingredients in large bowl. Stir brandy into whipped cream, then fold into ice cream mixture. Divide mixture among muffin cups. Freeze until firm, at least 15 minutes.

Hazelnut Semifreddo

Use leftover praline in other desserts.

8 servings

Hazelnut Praline
½ **cup sugar**
2 **tablespoons water**
½ **cup hazelnuts, toasted and husked**

Semifreddo
2⅔ **cups well-chilled whipping cream**
2 **tablespoons plus 2 teaspoons hazelnut or amaretto liqueur**

8 **egg yolks, room temperature**
10 **tablespoons sugar**

Red seedless grapes
1 **egg white, beaten to blend**
Sugar

Fresh mint sprigs

For praline: Grease baking sheet. Heat sugar and water in heavy small saucepan over low heat, swirling pan occasionally, until sugar dissolves. Increase heat and boil until light brown. Stir in hazelnuts. Return mixture to boil. Immediately pour onto prepared sheet, spreading thinly. Cool completely. Pulverize in processor or blender.

For semifreddo: Beat cream in large chilled bowl until beginning to thicken. Add liqueur and beat just until peaks form. Beat yolks with 10 tablespoons sugar in another large bowl until pale yellow and slowly dissolving ribbon forms when beaters are lifted. Gently fold in whipped cream and ⅓ cup praline. Spoon into serving glasses. Freeze at least 2 hours. (*Can be prepared 1 day ahead.*)

Dip grapes in egg white, then sugar, coating well. Let dry 30 minutes.

If semifreddo is frozen solid, let soften in refrigerator 30 minutes before serving. Garnish with grapes and mint.

Marsala Whipped Cream Tart with Fresh Figs

The filling goes well with any fruit.

6 servings

Crust
- ½ cup plus 2 tablespoons unbleached all purpose flour
- ¼ cup (½ stick) unsalted butter, cut into ½-inch pieces
- 3 tablespoons dry Marsala
- Pinch of salt

Zabaglione Filling
- 5 extra-large egg yolks, room temperature
- 5 tablespoons sugar
- ¼ cup dry Marsala
- ¼ cup light rum

- 5 fresh large figs, cut into ⅓-inch thick rounds
- 2 cups whipping cream, well chilled
- 2 tablespoons sugar
- 1 teaspoon powdered sugar

For crust: Sift flour onto work surface and arrange in mound. Place butter atop mound. Let stand until butter softens, about 30 minutes. Mix flour into butter with fingers, then rub between palms until thoroughly combined. Blend in Marsala and salt, using fork. Form dough into ball. Knead until smooth and elastic, about 2 minutes. Wrap in damp kitchen towel. Refrigerate at least 1 hour.

Preheat oven to 375°F. Butter 9- to 9½-inch tart pan. Knead dough on lightly floured surface 1 minute. Roll dough out on lightly floured surface into 12-inch round. Roll up onto rolling pin and unroll over prepared pan. Gently fit dough into pan. Trim overhanging pastry by rolling over edges. Finish edges. Pierce crust all over with fork. Line with foil, shiny side down. Fill with dried beans or rice. Bake 30 minutes. Remove beans and foil and continue baking until crust is light brown, about 19 minutes. Cool 1 hour. (*Can be prepared 1 day ahead.*)

For filling: Whisk yolks and sugar in top of double boiler until sugar dissolves and mixture is pale yellow. Gradually stir in Marsala and rum. Set over boiling water and whisk until mixture leaves path on back of spoon when finger is drawn across, about 4 minutes; do not boil. Pour into bowl and set plastic wrap directly onto surface of zabaglione; cool. Refrigerate until cold, about 30 minutes. (*Can be prepared 1 day ahead.*)

Preheat oven to 375°F. Spread zabaglione in crust. Bake 5 minutes. Cool.

Arrange fig slices around edge of tart. Beat cream until just beginning to thicken. Add sugar and powdered sugar and whip to soft peaks. Spoon into center of tart. Serve immediately.

Plum and Almond Tart

8 servings

Sweet Crust
- 2 cups sifted all purpose flour
- ¼ cup sugar
- ½ cup (1 stick) well-chilled unsalted butter
- 3 egg yolks
- ¾ teaspoon grated lemon peel
- 1½ to 2 tablespoons sweet white wine or water

Filling
- ½ cup sugar
- ½ cup unblanched almonds

- 2 tablespoons all purpose flour
- ¾ teaspoon cinnamon
- 6 egg whites, room temperature
- Pinch of cream of tartar
- Pinch of salt
- 1½ pounds slightly underripe red plums, quartered and pitted

For crust: Mix flour and sugar in large bowl. Cut in butter until coarse meal forms. Make well in center of dry ingredients. Add yolks, lemon peel and 1½ tablespoons wine to well; work into dry ingredients, adding more wine if necessary to bind dough. Gather into ball; flatten to disc. Wrap dough and refrigerate at least 30 minutes. (*Can be prepared 2 days ahead.*)

Roll dough out on lightly floured surface to ¼-inch-thick round. Transfer to 9 × 2½-inch springform pan. Trim edges. Refrigerate 1 hour.

Preheat oven to 375°F. Line crust with parchment; fill with dried beans or pie weights. Bake 10 minutes. Remove parchment and beans and bake crust until brown, about 15 minutes. Cool. Reduce temperature to 350°F.

For filling: Blend sugar, almonds, flour and cinnamon in processor until almonds are finely ground. Beat whites with cream of tartar and salt in large bowl until stiff but not dry. Gently fold in almond mixture, then plums.

Turn filling into crust. Bake until top is golden brown and knife inserted in center comes out clean, covering edges with foil if browning too quickly, about 45 minutes. Cool 15 minutes. Serve warm.

Lemon-Raisin Tart

6 servings

¾ cup golden raisins
¾ cup vodka

Crust
1½ cups unbleached all purpose flour
2 tablespoons sugar
Pinch of salt
6 tablespoons (¾ stick) well-chilled unsalted butter, cut into small pieces
3 tablespoons well-chilled solid vegetable shortening, cut into small pieces
3 to 4 tablespoons ice water

Filling
3 eggs
3 egg yolks
¾ cup plus 1 tablespoon sugar
⅔ cup fresh lemon juice, strained
3 tablespoons grated lemon peel

Thin lemon slices (optional)

Bring raisins and vodka to simmer over low heat. Remove from heat. Let stand at least 4 hours or overnight.

For crust: Combine flour, sugar and salt in processor. Cut in butter and shortening until mixture resembles coarse meal. With machine running, blend in ice water 1 tablespoon at a time until dough just starts to come together (do not form ball). Turn dough out onto lightly floured surface. Flatten into disc. Wrap in plastic. Refrigerate 30 minutes.

Roll dough out on lightly floured surface to thickness of ⅛ inch. Fit into 9-inch tart shell with removable bottom; trim edges. Chill shell 30 minutes.

Preheat oven to 400°F. Pierce shell with fork. Line with parchment or foil. Fill with dried beans or pie weights. Bake until pastry is set, about 10 minutes. Remove beans and foil. Bake until golden brown, about 10 minutes.

For filling: Preheat oven to 350°F. Drain raisins, reserving vodka. Whisk eggs and yolks in medium bowl. Stir in vodka, sugar, lemon juice and peel. Spread raisins in tart shell. Set shell in oven. Pour in filling. Bake until firm, 20 to 25 minutes. Cool completely on rack. Decorate with lemon slices.

Amor Polenta

6 servings

Cake

Butter
10 tablespoons butter, room temperature
2²/₃ cups sifted powdered sugar
1 teaspoon vanilla
2 eggs, room temperature
1 egg yolk, room temperature
1¼ cups cake flour, sifted
⅓ cup yellow cornmeal

¼ teaspoon salt
3 tablespoons powdered sugar

Sauce

12 ounces fresh or frozen raspberries
3 tablespoons orange liqueur
2 tablespoons powdered sugar

For cake: Preheat oven to 325°F. Butter and flour 10-inch Rehrucken (saddle loaf) pan or 8 × 4-inch loaf pan. Using electric mixer, cream 10 tablespoons butter with 2²/₃ cups powdered sugar and vanilla until smooth. Beat in eggs and yolk 1 at a time. Combine flour, cornmeal and salt. Gradually add to butter mixture and beat until well blended. Spoon batter into prepared pan. Bake until tester inserted in cake comes out clean, about 1¼ hours. Cool cake in pan 5 minutes. Unmold on rack. Sift 3 tablespoons powdered sugar over cake. Cool completely.

For sauce: Puree all ingredients in blender or processor. Press through fine sieve to eliminate seeds.

To serve, cut cake into thin slices Spoon sauce onto dessert plates. Top sauce with cake slices.

Zuccotto

8 to 10 servings

Cake

6 egg yolks, room temperature
1 cup powdered sugar
1 teaspoon vanilla
6 egg whites, room temperature
1 teaspoon salt

½ cup all purpose flour
½ cup potato flour
1 teaspoon cream of tartar

3 tablespoons Cognac
6 tablespoons Amaretto or Triple Sec liqueur

Cream Filling

3 envelopes unflavored gelatin
½ cup cold water

5 cups whipping cream
½ cup sugar
½ cup slivered almonds, toasted and coarsely chopped
½ cup hazelnuts, toasted, skinned and coarsely chopped
5 ounces semisweet chocolate chips
3 ounces semisweet chocolate, melted and cooled

2 tablespoons powdered sugar
2 tablespoons unsweetened cocoa powder

For cake: Preheat oven to 350°F. Generously butter and flour three 9-inch round cake pans.

Combine yolks, powdered sugar and vanilla in large bowl and beat until fluffy and lemon colored, about 10 minutes. Beat egg whites and salt in another bowl until stiff and glossy. Gently fold whites into yolks, blending well.

Sift flours and cream of tartar into another bowl. Fold into egg mixture, blending well. Transfer to prepared pans and bake layers until tester inserted in center comes out clean, about 25 minutes. Invert cake layers onto racks and let cool completely.

Line 2½-quart bowl with plastic wrap, allowing 4- to 5-inch overlap. Trim two cake layers to fit bottom and sides of bowl and arrange in place. Sprinkle with 1½ tablespoons Cognac and 3 tablespoons liqueur.

For filling: Combine gelatin with water in heat-resistant cup and mix until gelatin is softened. Place cup in simmering water and heat until gelatin is completely liquefied, about 2 to 3 minutes. Using electric mixer, beat cream in large bowl until almost thickened. Gradually add sugar and continue beating until stiff. Pour gelatin into center of cream and blend well. Fold in nuts and chocolate chips. Spoon *half* of cream into another bowl and gently fold in melted chocolate.

To assemble: Spread plain whipped cream mixture over cake in bottom and sides of mold. Fill center with chocolate cream mixture. Cover with remaining cake layer, trimming as necessary. Sprinkle with remaining Cognac and liqueur. Fold plastic over cake, pressing lightly and sealing tightly. Refrigerate at least 2 hours or overnight.

Invert mold onto serving platter and discard plastic wrap. Refrigerate. Just before serving, combine powdered sugar and cocoa in mixing bowl and sprinkle over top of cake.

Mary Tassiello's Ricotta Cake

8 to 12 servings

Pastry
1½ cups all purpose flour
¼ teaspoon salt
6 tablespoons (¾ stick) well-chilled unsalted butter, cut into small pieces
2 tablespoons well-chilled solid vegetable shortening, cut into small pieces
1 egg yolk
2 tablespoons (or more) ice water

Ricotta Filling
1½ pounds whole milk ricotta cheese
2 tablespoons grated lemon peel
1 tablespoon grated orange peel
1 tablespoon all purpose flour
1 tablespoon vanilla
⅓ teaspoon salt
1 cup sugar
4 eggs, room temperature

½ cup whipping cream
Pinch of freshly grated nutmeg

For pastry: Combine flour and salt in large bowl. Add butter and shortening and mix quickly with fingertips or pastry blender until mixture resembles coarse meal. Beat yolk and 2 tablespoons ice water in small bowl to blend. Add to flour mixture and blend until dough just holds together, sprinkling with additional ice water as necessary; do not overmix or pastry will be tough. Lightly flour hands. Shape dough into ball, then flatten into 1-inch-thick disc. Wrap in waxed paper or plastic and refrigerate until well chilled, at least 1 hour.

Lightly grease 9 × 1½-inch round cake pan with removable bottom. Roll dough out on lightly floured surface to 12-inch circle ⅛ inch thick. Fit dough into pan, pressing gently. Trim edges and crimp decoratively if desired. Freeze until firm, about 30 minutes.

Preheat oven to 425°F. Bake crust until set and golden, about 20 minutes.

For filling: Preheat oven to 350°F. Combine cheese, lemon and orange peels, flour, vanilla and salt in large bowl of electric mixer and blend until as smooth as possible. Beat sugar with eggs in another bowl until pale yellow and slowly dissolving ribbon forms when beaters are lifted, about 7 minutes. Add eggs to cheese mixture and blend thoroughly. Pour filling into crust. Bake until filling is firm, 50 to 60 minutes. Cool on rack 30 minutes.

To serve, whip cream to soft peaks. Spoon cream into pastry bag fitted with star tip. Pipe 8 to 12 rosettes around rim of cake. Sprinkle rosettes with freshly grated nutmeg. Serve cake at room temperature.

Cherry Ricotta Cake

14 servings

Sponge Cake
 6 eggs, room temperature
 ³/₄ cup sugar
 ¹/₂ teaspoon salt
 2 tablespoons vanilla
 1 cup sifted cake flour

Filling
 8 ounces imported bittersweet (not unsweetened) or semisweet chocolate, broken into pieces
 2 pounds fresh ricotta cheese
 1 cup powdered sugar
 5 tablespoons dark rum

Rum Syrup
 ¹/₂ cup sugar
 ¹/₄ cup water
 ¹/₂ cup dark rum

 1 16¹/₂-ounce can pitted dark cherries, drained, or 1 12-ounce jar Morello cherry jam

 Chocolate curls (optional)

For cake: Position rack in lower third of oven and preheat to 350°F. Butter 10-inch springform pan. Line bottom with parchment. Using electric mixer, beat eggs well. Beat in sugar 1 tablespoon at a time. Add salt and beat until pale yellow and slowly dissolving ribbon forms when beaters are lifted. Mix in vanilla. Sift flour onto batter and fold in gently but quickly. Pour batter into prepared pan. Bake until tester inserted in center of cake comes out clean, about 25 minutes. Cool on rack. (*Can be prepared 1 day ahead. Wrap tightly and store at room temperature.*)

For filling: Finely chop chocolate in processor using on/off turns. Sift chocolate to separate powder and bits. Blend ricotta and sugar in processor until smooth. Mix in rum. Transfer ¹/₄ cup ricotta mixture to small bowl; cover and refrigerate. Fold chocolate bits into remaining filling. Reserve powdered chocolate for garnish.

For syrup: Cook sugar and water in heavy small saucepan over low heat, swirling pan occasionally, until sugar dissolves. Mix in rum.

Remove parchment from cake. Cut cake into 3 layers. Place bottom layer, cut side up, in clean 10-inch springform pan. Brush generously with rum syrup. Spread half of filling over cake. Top with half of cherries. Place middle cake layer atop cherries. Brush generously with syrup. Spread with remaining filling, then remaining cherries. Place last layer in pan, cut side down. Brush generously with syrup. Chill uncovered at least 3 hours or overnight.

Remove pan sides. Spread cake sides with reserved ¹/₄ cup ricotta mixture. Sprinkle top and sides with powdered chocolate. Gently press chocolate curls into sides; mound a few in center of cake. Let cake stand at room temperature 30 minutes before serving.

Almond Cake with Tortoni

Tortoni—that marvelous Italian treat of ice cream, maraschino cherries and almonds—gets dressed up in this easy dessert. Amaretto is a nice change from the more usual rum.

8 servings

Almond Cake
- 3 eggs, room temperature
- ²/₃ cup sugar
- 1½ teaspoons vanilla
- ½ cup (1 stick) unsalted butter, room temperature
- ⅓ cup all purpose flour
- ¾ cup ground blanched almonds

Tortoni
- ⅓ cup chopped raisins
- ⅓ cup chopped dates
- ⅓ cup chopped semisweet chocolate chips
- ⅓ cup chopped maraschino cherries
- ⅓ cup chopped toasted almonds
- ⅓ cup amaretto liqueur
- 2 tablespoons maraschino cherry juice
- 1 quart vanilla ice cream, softened

Raspberry Coulis
- 6 10-ounce packages unsweetened frozen raspberries, thawed and drained
- ⅓ cup sugar

  Mint leaves

For cake: Preheat oven to 350°F. Butter and flour 9 × 13-inch cake pan. Using electric mixer, beat eggs, sugar and vanilla until thick and pale. Cream butter in another bowl. Stir about ½ cup egg mixture into butter. Gently fold flour and almonds alternately into egg mixture. Fold in creamed butter mixture. Turn into prepared pan. Bake until tester inserted in center comes out clean, about 30 minutes. Cool 10 minutes in pan. Invert almond cake onto rack and cool completely.

For tortoni: Combine first 7 ingredients. Stir in ice cream. Freeze until firm.

For coulis: Puree raspberries and sugar in processor. Strain mixture through fine sieve to eliminate seeds.

To assemble: Using 3-inch flower-shaped cutter, cut out 8 cake flowers. Spoon ⅓ cup raspberry coulis onto each dessert plate. Top with cake flower. Set mint leaves between petals. Spoon tortoni atop cake.

Italian Almond Cake

10 to 12 servings

- 1 tablespoon butter (for pan)
- 8 ounces almond paste
- 6 eggs, separated, room temperature
- 1 teaspoon vanilla
- ½ teaspoon almond extract
  Pinch of salt
- ½ cup sugar
- ½ cup all purpose flour
- 1 teaspoon baking powder
- 1½ cups whipping cream
- ½ cup powdered sugar
- 2 tablespoons crème de almond liqueur* or grenadine
- 6 ounces semisweet chocolate

Preheat oven to 350°F. Butter 9-inch springform pan. Beat almond paste and egg yolks in large bowl of electric mixer until well blended. Mix in vanilla and almond extract. Beat egg whites and salt in another large bowl until soft peaks form. Add sugar about 1 tablespoon at a time, beating until stiff but not dry. Fold ⅓ of whites into yolk mixture to lighten. Gently fold in remaining whites. Combine flour and baking powder in small bowl. Fold into egg mixture 2 tablespoons at a time, being careful not to deflate mixture. Pour batter into prepared pan, smoothing top. Bake until top is browned and tester inserted in center comes out clean, about 30 minutes. Cool on rack. Cake will fall slightly in center. (*Can be prepared ahead. Wrap in plastic and refrigerate. Bring to room temperature before frosting.)*

Invert cake onto serving platter. Whip cream to soft peaks in large bowl. Blend in powdered sugar. Set aside ½ cup. Mix liqueur into remaining cream. Spread colored cream decoratively over top and sides of cake. Spoon reserved cream into pastry bag fitted with star tip. Pipe tiny rosettes around top rim and base of cake. Melt chocolate in top of double boiler over hot water, stirring occasionally. Line baking sheet with plastic wrap. Pour chocolate onto plastic and spread with spatula to thickness of about ⅛ inch. Let cool completely. Cut chocolate into heart shapes using cookie cutters. Garnish top of cake with chocolate. Chill. Serve at room temperature.

*Crème de almond (also called crème de noyaux) is red in color and will lend pink tint to whipped cream.

Zucchini Tube Cake

This cake is a delicious variation of zucchini bread.

12 servings

4 eggs, room temperature
2 cups sugar
1⅓ cups vegetable oil
3 cups shredded unpeeled zucchini (about 3 medium)
3 cups all purpose flour
1½ teaspoons baking soda
1½ teaspoons baking powder
1½ teaspoons cinnamon
1 teaspoon salt
1½ cups walnut halves, chopped (about ½ pound)
1 cup golden raisins
1 cup whipping cream, whipped (garnish)

Preheat oven to 350°F. Generously butter 10 × 4¼-inch tube pan. Beat eggs in large bowl until well blended. Stir in sugar. Blend in oil. Beat 1 minute. Add zucchini and mix well. Sift together flour, baking soda, baking powder, cinnamon and salt. Fold into zucchini mixture. Stir in nuts and raisins. Turn batter into prepared pan. Bake until tester inserted near center comes out clean, about 1 hour. Cool about 20 minutes. Invert cake onto dessert platter. Serve with whipped cream.

Zabaglione Cake with Chocolate Frosting

8 to 10 servings

Cake
8 eggs, separated, room temperature
1 cup plus 2 tablespoons sugar
1 teaspoon vanilla
1 teaspoon cream of tartar
Pinch of salt
1 cup sifted (3 times) all purpose flour

Zabaglione
6 egg yolks, room temperature
¾ cup sugar
1 cup dry Marsala

Frosting
½ cup whipping cream
½ cup sugar
2½ ounces unsweetened chocolate
¼ cup (½ stick) unsalted butter, room temperature
½ teaspoon vanilla

Strawberries

For cake: Preheat oven to 350°F. Grease and flour 9 × 13-inch ovenproof glass pan. Using electric mixer, beat yolks with ⅓ of sugar until thick and pale and ribbon forms when beaters are lifted. Blend in vanilla. Using clean dry beaters, beat whites with cream of tartar and salt until stiff but not dry. Gradually add ⅓ of sugar, beating until whites cling to sides of bowl. Gently fold yolk mixture into whites. Combine flour and remaining ⅓ of sugar. Fold flour mixture carefully into egg mixture. Turn into prepared pan. Bake until cake springs back when lightly touched, about 30 minutes. Invert cake in pan onto 2 cans and cool completely.

Remove cake from pan. Using long serrated knife, cut cake in half down center. Wrap in foil. Freeze 1 day.

Cut each half horizontally into 3 layers. Set all 6 layers aside.

For zabaglione: Place yolks in heavy medium saucepan. Gradually add sugar and whisk until thick and pale. Whisk in Marsala in slow stream. Set over medium heat and beat until slowly dissolving ribbon forms when whisk is lifted; do not overcook or custard will curdle. Set 1 cake layer on platter. Immediately spread with ⅓ cup zabaglione. Repeat layering with remaining cake and zabaglione, pressing down gently, ending with cake.

For frosting: Heat cream and sugar in heavy small saucepan until sugar dissolves, swirling pan occasionally. Bring to boil, stirring constantly. Reduce heat and simmer very gently until thick and syrupy, adjusting heat so liquid is barely shaking, about 10 minutes. Remove from heat. Add chocolate and stir until smooth. Stir in butter and vanilla. Chill until spreadable.

Spread top and sides of cake with frosting. Refrigerate overnight. Bring to room temperature before serving. Garnish with strawberries.

Cocoa Custard Cake

For best results, make this custard cake one to two days ahead.

8 servings

Sponge Cake
- 4 eggs, separated, room temperature
- ¾ cup sugar
- ¾ cup all purpose flour sifted with 1 teaspoon baking powder
- ¼ teaspoon lemon or vanilla extract

  Pinch of cream of tartar

Custard
- 4 egg yolks
- ¾ cup sugar
- 3 tablespoons all purpose flour
- 2 cups milk
- 2 small lemon peel strips
- 1 teaspoon vanilla extract

- 2 tablespoons finely chopped toasted blanched almonds
- 1½ tablespoons unsweetened cocoa powder
  Dark rum
  Orange liqueur
- 6 to 8 ladyfingers, halved vertically
- 2 blanched almonds

For sponge cake: Preheat oven to 350°F. Lightly butter and flour 9-inch round cake pan. Beat yolks in mixing bowl until light in color. Gradually beat in ½ cup sugar and continue beating until mixture forms slowly dissolving ribbon when beaters are lifted. Fold in flour in 3 batches; batter will be stiff. Blend in lemon or vanilla extract.

Beat whites and cream of tartar in mixing bowl until soft peaks form. Gradually beat in remaining ¼ cup sugar until whites are stiff but not dry. Gently fold into yolk mixture. Pour into prepared pan. Bake until top of cake is golden brown and tester inserted in center comes out clean, 35 to 40 minutes. Immediately invert onto rack and cool completely (do not remove pan). Run thin-bladed knife around edge of cake and invert onto platter.

For custard: Whisk yolks, sugar and flour in heavy large saucepan until smooth. Gradually whisk in milk. And lemon peel. Stir over medium-low heat until mixture just boils. Turn into nonaluminum bowl, discarding lemon peel. Stir in vanilla. Cool.

To assemble: Divide custard among 3 bowls. Stir almonds into 1 and cocoa powder into another. Cut cake into 3 layers using long serrated knife. Set 1 layer on platter. Sprinkle generously with rum and spread with almond custard. Top with second layer. Sprinkle generously with rum and spread with plain custard. Cover with remaining layer. Sprinkle generously with orange liqueur and spread with almost all cocoa custard, smoothing remainder around sides of cake. Sprinkle flat side of ladyfingers lightly with rum or orange liqueur. Press ladyfingers around sides of cake rounded side out. Set almonds atop cake for decoration.

La Gubana

A rich fruit and nut coffee cake that is traditionally served with a spoonful of slivovitz poured over each slice.

10 to 12 servings

¾ cup warm milk (105°F to 115°F)
3 envelopes dry yeast
5 cups unbleached all purpose flour (or more)

¾ cup sugar
½ cup (1 stick) butter, melted and cooled
3 eggs, lightly beaten
2 teaspoons salt
Additional milk (room temperature), optional

6 ounces golden raisins
3 ounces mixed dried fruit (such as apricots, apples, peaches, pears)
4 ounces shelled hazelnuts, skinned*

1 ounce blanched almonds
1 ounce pine nuts
3 tablespoons butter
1 tablespoon fresh breadcrumbs
1 to 2 tablespoons brandy
1 egg, separated

1 egg yolk, lightly beaten
Sugar
Slivovitz or other plum brandy

Butter large baking sheet. Combine ¾ cup warm milk with yeast in large bowl of electric mixer and let stand 10 minutes, stirring occasionally. Add 1 cup flour and beat 2 minutes. Cover bowl with damp towel and let rise in warm draft-free area until mixture is light and filled with bubbles, about 1 hour.

Add 4 cups flour, sugar, melted butter, eggs and salt and mix until dough is soft but not sticky, adding more flour or milk as necessary. Knead 5 minutes in mixer fitted with dough hook. Transfer dough to lightly floured surface and knead 5 minutes by hand. Return dough to bowl. Cover and let rise in warm draft-free area until doubled in volume, about 1½ to 2 hours.

Meanwhile, steam raisins and dried fruit over boiling water until softened, about 5 minutes. Drain well. Finely chop hazelnuts, almonds and dried fruit. Transfer to large bowl. Add raisins and pine nuts. Melt butter in small saucepan over medium heat. Add breadcrumbs and cook until browned, stirring constantly, about 3 minutes. Add browned breadcrumbs to fruit mixture and stir well. Mix in brandy and egg yolk.

Punch dough down; let rest 5 minutes. Transfer to lightly floured surface. Roll out into rectangle about 12 inches wide and 24 inches long. Beat reserved egg white in small bowl until stiff peaks form. Gently stir into filling. Spread filling over dough, leaving narrow border around edges. Roll dough up lengthwise, pinching seam to seal filling. Roll dough cylinder back and forth gently with hands until about 36 inches long. Transfer to prepared baking sheet. Coil into spiral, tucking end in tightly. Drape damp towel over dough and let rise in warm draft-free area until doubled, about 1 hour.

Preheat oven to 400°F. Brush surface of dough with egg yolk and sprinkle with sugar. Bake 15 minutes. Reduce oven temperature to 375°F and continue baking until cake sounds hollow when tapped, about 30 minutes (check after 5 minutes; if top is browning too quickly, cover loosely with foil). Cool on rack. Serve either warm or at room temperature. Sprinkle each slice with 1 to 2 teaspoons slivovitz if desired.

*To skin hazelnuts, toast in 300°F oven 15 minutes. Rub skins off with towel.

Panettone

Makes 2 loaves

    ¾ cup milk
    ½ cup (1 stick) unsalted butter
    ½ cup sugar
    1 teaspoon salt
    ¼ cup warm water (105°F to 115°F)
    2 envelopes dry yeast
    1 egg
    4 egg yolks

    4½ to 5 cups (about) sifted all
       purpose flour
    1 cup chopped candied citron
    ¾ cup golden raisins

    1 tablespoon powdered sugar

Butter two 1-quart round ovenproof glass baking dishes (3 inches high, 7 inches in diameter). Combine milk, butter, sugar and salt in small saucepan and bring just to scalding point over medium heat. Cool to 105°F to 115°F. Combine warm water and yeast in processor and mix briefly using 1 or 2 on/off turns. Add milk mixture and blend 5 to 10 seconds. Add egg and combine using on/off turns. Add yolks one at a time, mixing with on/off turns after each addition. Add 1 cup flour and process 5 seconds. Scrape sides of work bowl; process 10 seconds. Repeat with 2 more cups of flour. Transfer dough to warmed large bowl. Stir in citron and raisins. Add 1 cup flour (dough will be very stiff). Turn dough out onto lightly floured pastry cloth (or other surface) and work in enough remaining flour to make soft but manageable dough. Knead until shiny and elastic, about 2 to 3 minutes. Shape dough into ball. Transfer to warmed buttered bowl, turning to coat all sides. Cover with dry cloth and let rise in warm draft-free area until doubled, 2½ hours.

Punch dough down. Transfer to lightly floured pastry cloth and knead 2 to 3 minutes. Divide dough in half; shape each into ball. Transfer to prepared baking dishes. Cover with dry cloth and let rise in warm draft-free area until doubled in volume, 2½ hours.

Preheat oven to 400°F. Bake loaves 10 minutes. Reduce oven temperature to 350°F and continue baking until loaves are richly browned and sound hollow when tapped, about 20 minutes. Cool 5 minutes in dishes (set on sides). Remove loaves from dishes and cool completely. Sift powdered sugar over tops of loaves before serving. (*Panettone can be frozen up to 3 months. Wrap tightly in foil or plastic wrap.*)

Strawberry Panini

6 servings

Cookies
- ½ cup (1 stick) unsalted butter, cut into small pieces
- ½ cup sugar
- 2 egg yolks
- ¼ teaspoon vanilla
  Pinch of salt
- 1⅓ cups sifted all purpose flour

Topping
- 2½ pints small strawberries
- ¼ cup sugar
- 2 tablespoons orange liqueur

Powdered sugar
Whipped cream

For cookies: Cream butter and sugar in processor, about 1 minute, stopping to scrape down sides of bowl. Blend in yolks, vanilla and salt. With machine running, gradually add flour through feed tube and mix just to incorporate. Turn dough out onto surface. Cut in half. Wrap each piece in plastic; flatten into discs. Refrigerate dough for several hours or overnight.

Butter baking sheets. Roll 1 piece of dough out between 2 sheets of waxed paper to thickness of ⅛ inch. Cut out 6 rounds using 3½- to 4-inch fluted cutter. Using spatula, transfer round to prepared sheets. Repeat with remaining dough. Refrigerate until firm.

Preheat oven to 350°F. Bake cookies until pale golden about 8 minutes. Cool cookies completely on racks.

For topping: Set aside 6 strawberries for garnish. Hull remaining strawberries. Set aside 1½ pints strawberries of equal size. Puree remaining berries with sugar and liqueur in processor. Transfer to bowl. Cover and chill.

To assemble: Just before serving, set 1 cookie on each of 6 dessert plates. Arrange ⅙ of reserved 1½ pints strawberries hulled side down atop each. Set another cookie atop strawberries. Sift powdered sugar over. Surround with some of strawberry puree. Garnish panini with reserved 6 strawberries and serve. Pass whipped cream separately.

Sweet Semolina Diamonds

Semolina flour, made from durum wheat, is the basis of many pastas. It is combined here with sugar and all purpose flour to produce a slightly sweet, crunchy rum-raisin cookie.

Makes about 3 dozen

- 1 cup light rum
- 1 cup seedless golden raisins

- 4 egg yolks, room temperature
- 1 cup sugar

- 2 cups all purpose flour
- 1½ cups semolina flour
- 1 cup (2 sticks) unsalted butter, melted and cooled

- 1 teaspoon vanilla
  Grated peel of 1 lemon
- ¼ teaspoon salt
- ½ cup pine nuts
- 2 tablespoons powdered sugar

Combine rum and raisins in small bowl and set aside several hours (or overnight) to plump. Drain raisins, reserving liquid. Pat raisins dry.

Preheat oven to 375°F. Generously butter baking sheets. Beat yolks and sugar in large bowl of electric mixer until slowly dissolving ribbon forms when beaters are lifted, 7 minutes.

Combine flours and gradually mix into egg mixture. Blend in melted butter, vanilla, lemon peel, salt and reserved raisin liquid. Fit mixer with dough hook or turn dough out onto lightly floured surface. Knead until smooth, about 5 minutes. Sprinkle raisins and nuts over dough and continue kneading just until incorporated. Lightly flour work surface again. Roll dough out to thickness of

¹/₃ inch. Using very sharp knife, cut dough diagonally in opposite directions to form diamonds. Transfer diamonds to baking sheets, spacing evenly. Bake until cookies are lightly colored, about 20 minutes. Serve warm or at room temperature. Store in air-tight container. Sprinkle with powdered sugar before serving.

Sweet Ricotta-filled Pastries

Makes about 28

Pastry
- 2 cups all purpose flour
- 2 tablespoons sugar
- ¹/₄ teaspoon salt
- 4 tablespoons lard, well chilled
- 2 eggs, room temperature
- 2 tablespoons dry white wine

Ricotta-Fruit Filling
- 1 cup ricotta cheese
- ¹/₂ cup powdered sugar
- ¹/₂ cup hazelnuts, roasted, husked and chopped
- ¹/₄ cup diced candied fruit
- 2 ounces unsweetened, bittersweet or semisweet chocolate, chopped
- 1 teaspoon cinnamon

Lard or vegetable oil (for deep frying)
Vanilla powdered sugar* or powdered sugar

For pastry: Sift flour, sugar and salt onto work surface. Work in lard with fingertips until coarse meal forms. Make well in center. Add eggs and wine to well and blend with fork. Gradually draw flour from inner edge of well into center until all flour is incorporated. Knead until smooth dough forms, about 6 minutes. (Can also be prepared with heavy-duty mixer. Knead about 3 minutes.) Cover dough with towel and let rest 30 minutes. (*Can be prepared 1 day ahead. Wrap tightly and refrigerate. Bring pastry to room temperature before continuing with recipe.*)

For filling: Using electric mixer, beat ricotta and ¹/₂ cup sugar until smooth. Fold in nuts, fruit, chocolate and cinnamon. (*Can be prepared 1 day ahead. Cover and refrigerate. Bring to room temperature before continuing.*)

Roll out half of pastry on lightly floured surface to thickness of ¹/₈ inch. Cut out 2¹/₂- to 3-inch circles using fluted cookie cutter or glass.** Place heaping teaspoon of filling in center of 1 round. Moisten edge and top with another round. Press edges together to seal. Repeat with remaining pastry and filling. (*Can be prepared ahead. Arrange on waxed paper-lined baking sheet and wrap tightly. Chill overnight or freeze 2 weeks. Do not thaw before cooking.*)

Melt lard in deep saucepan to depth of 1 inch and heat to 350°F. Add pastries in batches (do not crowd) and cook until golden brown, about 40 seconds per side. Drain on paper towels. Sprinkle with vanilla sugar. Serve warm or at room temperature.

*Combine 1 vanilla bean and 1 pound powdered sugar in jar. Seal and let stand at least 1 week to develop flavor.

**Can also be formed into half-moon shape. Cut out 3¹/₂- to 4-inch rounds, using fluted cookie cutter or glass. Place rounded teaspoon filling in center of each, brush edges with water, fold in half and press to seal. Cook as above.

Sister Bea's White Wine Pastry Bows with Honey

Makes about 18 dozen

¼ cup water
3 tablespoons Sauternes, dry Sherry or Chablis
3 tablespoons vegetable oil
2 cups all purpose flour

2 cups vegetable oil (for frying)
1 cup honey
Powdered sugar

Combine water, wine and 3 tablespoons oil in small saucepan and bring to boil over high heat. Let boil to remove raw wine flavor, 3 to 5 minutes. Arrange flour in mound on lightly floured surface. Make well in center of flour. Carefully pour hot liquid into well. Gradually mix flour into liquid with fork. Knead dough until smooth and soft, about 5 minutes. Cover with damp towel and let rest 10 minutes. (*Dough can be made ahead and refrigerated. Bring to room temperature before continuing with recipe.*)

Divide dough in half. Cover 1 half with damp towel. Roll remaining half out on lightly floured surface into paper-thin sheets. Using fluted pastry wheel, cut dough into 1 × 1½-inch strips. Pinch strips in center to form bows. Heat oil in deep large skillet over medium-high heat to 375°F to 400°F. Add pastry bows in batches (do not crowd) and fry until golden on both sides. Remove from skillet using slotted spoon and drain on paper towels. Repeat with remaining dough.

Warm honey in deep large heavy skillet over medium-low heat. Gently add bows to honey in batches (do not crowd), coating evenly. Using slotted spoon, transfer bows to rack set over baking sheet and let drain. Store in airtight container, separating layers with waxed paper. Sprinkle with powdered sugar before serving.

Fried Zeppole

Potato-based "doughnuts" that are deep fried and drizzled with honey.

Makes 18

1¼ pounds small baking potatoes
2 tablespoons yeast
¼ cup warm milk (105°F to 115°F)
3½ cups (or more) unbleached all purpose flour
¼ teaspoon salt
Vegetable oil
Warm honey

3 tablespoons unsalted butter, melted
4 egg yolks

Boil potatoes until tender, about 20 minutes; do not pierce to test for doneness. Drain. Toss potatoes over low heat to dry completely. Peel immediately. Sieve; you should have about 4 cups. (*Can be prepared 1 day ahead. Cool completely, cover and refrigerate. Bring to room temperature before using.*)

Sprinkle yeast over milk in medium bowl and let stand until dissolved; stir to blend. Stir in ⅔ cup flour and knead until dough comes together, about 5 minutes. Grease and flour large bowl. Add dough, turning to coat entire surface. Cover and let stand in warm draft-free area until increased by 1½ times, approximately 1 hour.

Combine remaining flour and salt in mixer bowl. Add potatoes and butter and beat 5 minutes. Add yolks and beat 2 minutes. Beat yeast ball into dough, about 8 minutes; dough should be very soft and slightly sticky. If too sticky, add

1 to 2 tablespoons flour. Transfer dough to bowl lined with floured cloth. Cover and let rise in warm draft-free area until increased by half, about 2 hours.

Divide dough into 18 pieces. Roll each piece into 8-inch rope. Shape each into ring with 1-inch overlap where ends meet. Fold ends over and press to seal. Arrange on floured cloth.

Heat about 2 inches of oil in deep fryer to 270°F. Fry rings in batches (do not crowd) until golden brown, turning frequently, about 6 minutes. Remove using slotted utensil and drain on paper towels. Arrange on platter. Drizzle with honey. Serve immediately.

Calabrian Fried Bread Dessert

Makes about 30

1 recipe Italian Country Bread dough (see page 45)

Oil for deep frying

Sugar
Honey or jam

Pinch off pieces of dough slightly larger than golf balls. Flour hands lightly. Pat dough pieces between palms into flat, thin rounds about 3½ inches in diameter. (*Can be shaped 1 to 2 hours ahead. Arrange rounds on baking sheets and cover with towel. Pat dough flat before frying.*)

Heat oil in deep fryer or large saucepan to 360°F. Add dough in batches and fry until deep golden, turning once. Drain on paper towels. Sprinkle bread generously with sugar. Serve immediately with honey or jam.

🍐 Index

Credits and Acknowledgments

The following people contributed the recipes included in this book:

Bruce Aidells
Jean Anderson
Paola Bagnatori
Nancy Barocci
Nancy Verde Barr
Beth Boring
Patricia Brooks
Giuliano Bugialli
Bobby and Laura Cadwallader
Cafe Giovanni, Denver, Colorado
Anna Teresa Callen
Elaine Colgan
Diane Darrow
Jamie Davies
Deirdre Davis
Anita and Paul DeDomenico
Claudia Ebeling
Joe Famularo
Shelley Gillette
Freddi Greenberg
Bess Greenstone
Cathy and Don Hagen
Jane Helsel Joseph
Karen Kaplan
Kristine Kidd
La Bruschetta, Los Angeles, California
Heidi Landers

Le Cirque, New York, New York
Faye Levy
Mimmetta Lo Monte
Lofurno's, Seattle, Washington
Abby Mandel
Dani Manilla
Mary Manilla
Tom Maresca
Linda Marino
Mario's, Nashville, Tennessee
Michael McLaughlin
Shirley Metropoulos
Jefferson and Jinx Morgan
Doris Muscatine
Joanne O'Donnell
Park Hotel, Siena, Italy
Fenella Pearson
Pat and Steve Pepe
Elizabeth Riely
Franco and Margaret Romagnoli
Betty Rosbottom
David Rosengarten
Arlene and Lou Sarappo
Richard Sax
Jerry Slaby
Shirley Slater
Tallgrass Restaurant, Lockport, Illinois

The Elms, Saratoga Springs, New York
Vista International's American Harvest,
  New York, New York
Jan Weimer
Jan Wilton
Louise Wright

Additional text was supplied by:
Karen Kaplan and MaryJane Bescoby

Special thanks to:

Editorial Staff:
  Angeline Vogl
  MaryJane Bescoby

Graphics Staff:
  Bernard Rotondo
  Gloriane Harris

Rights and Permissions:
  Karen Legier

Indexer:
  Rose Grant

The Knapp Press
is a wholly owned subsidiary of
KNAPP COMMUNICATIONS CORPORATION.

Composition by Andresen Typographics, Tucson, Arizona

This book is set in Sabon, a face designed by Jan Teischold in 1967 and based on early
fonts engraved by Garamond and Granjon.